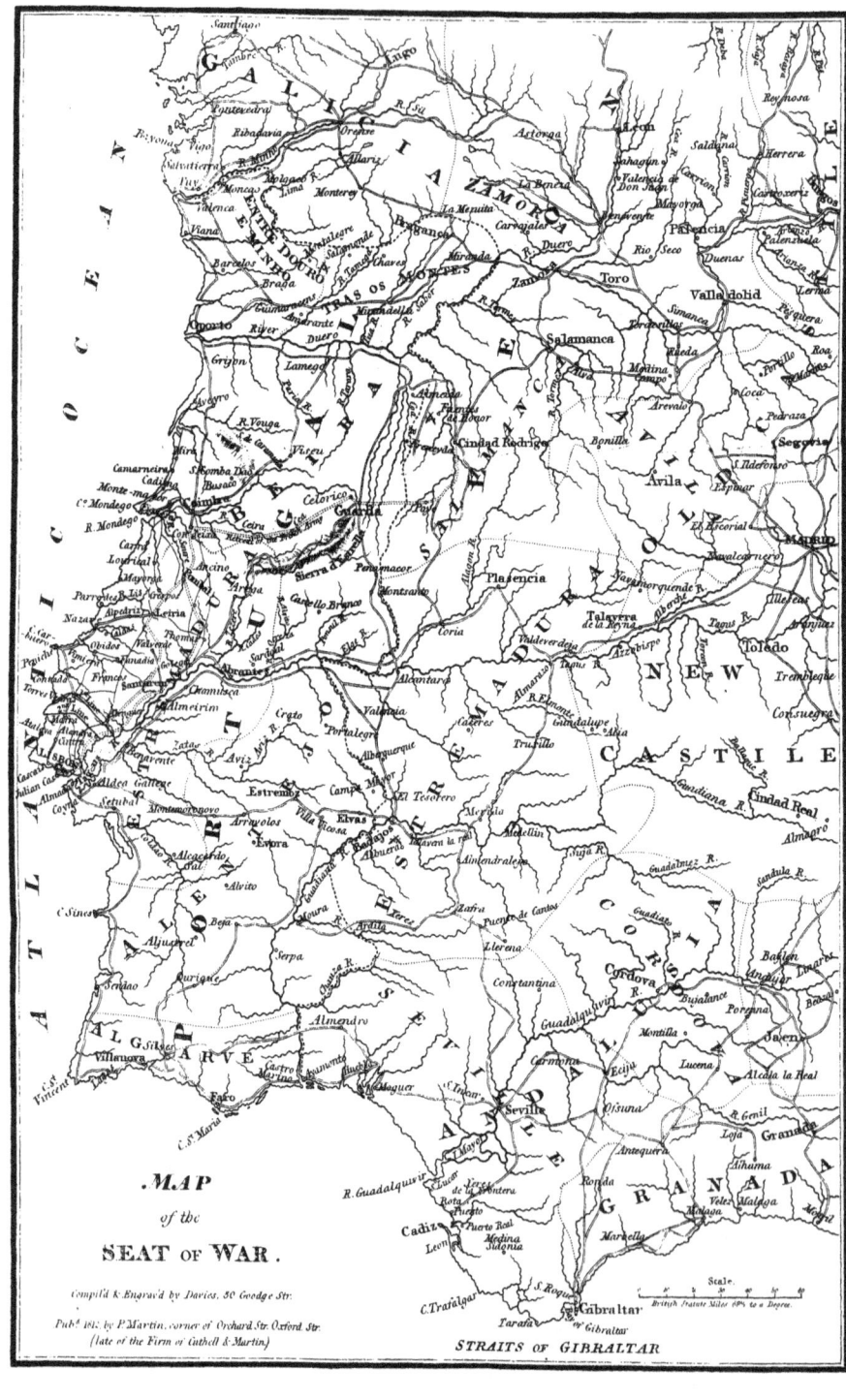

A NARRATIVE

OF THE

PRINCIPAL EVENTS

OF

THE CAMPAIGNS

OF

1809, 1810, & 1811,

IN

SPAIN AND PORTUGAL;

INTERSPERSED

WITH REMARKS

ON

LOCAL SCENERY AND MANNERS.

In a Series of Letters.

BY CAPTAIN WILLIAM STOTHERT,

ADJUTANT

THIRD FOOT GUARDS.

1812.

The Naval & Military Press Ltd

in association with

The National Army Museum, London

Published jointly by

The Naval & Military Press Ltd
Unit 10 Ridgewood Industrial Park,
Uckfield, East Sussex,
TN22 5QE England

Tel: +44 (0) 1825 749494
Fax: +44 (0) 1825 765701

www.naval-military-press.com
www.military-genealogy.com
www.militarymaproom.com

and

The National Army Museum, London
www.national-army-museum.ac.uk

In reprinting in facsimile from the original, any imperfections are inevitably reproduced and the quality may fall short of modern type and cartographic standards.

INTRODUCTION.

The following Letters have been arranged for publication nearly in their original form. In relating the circumstances of these eventful campaigns, the Writer has avoided offering any opinion on the policy of Great Britain in the aid afforded to the Peninsula, and the manner in which that aid has been applied. These pages will be found to contain, simply, a soldier's journal of the operations he has witnessed, of the marches he has performed, interspersed with occasional remarks on the manners and customs, and the local scenery of countries, which from the difficulties of travelling are less known than the rest of the continent. He is aware that many of his observations will not have even the recommendation of novelty, but where he may appear diffuse in his description of subjects not of a military nature, he relies on the indulgence of his readers.

INTRODUCTION.

The marches of the army have only been generally touched upon, the Writer confining himself principally to the route of the 1st division, and sometimes only to that of the battalion in which he served; but he has not omitted to detail occasionally, the movements of the whole, where he has had an opportunity of doing so with accuracy.

In a narrative of this nature, the Writer has denied himself the gratification of expatiating upon the well known gallantry of British troops, and the skill and military talents of the leaders under whom they fought. Their merits will be best appreciated in the hearts of a grateful country; and the historian when recording in his brightest page the BATTLE of TALAVERA, will not fail to transmit to an admiring posterity, a faithful detail of the splended atchievements and deeds of noble prowess displayed by the warriors of Britain throughout every trying hour of that memorable day!

CONTENTS.

LETTER I.

The Expedition Sails from Portsmouth.—Separated in a Gale of Wind, re-assembles at Cork.—Refused permission to dis-embark at Cadiz.—Arrival in the Tagus - - - 1

LETTER II.

Short Account of Lisbon.—The Churches, Aqueduct, &c. Reported situation of the French Armies under Marshals Soult and Victor - - - - - - - - 8

LETTER III.

The Guards March to Saccavem.—Sir John Craddock moves his Head-quarters to Lumiar.—Account received of Marshal Soult having taken Oporto.—Marshal Beresford sets out for Thomar - - - - - - - - 14

LETTER IV.

Continue their March through Alhandra, Carregada, and Alcoentre to Riomayor.—Description of the Country on the Route - - - - - - - - - 17

LETTER V.

Convent of St. Dominick at Batalha Leyria.—Sir John Craddock takes leave of the Army.—Bishop's Palace, &c. - 21

CONTENTS.

LETTER VI.

The Army assembles at Coimbra.—Description of that City.—Camoens.—Monastery of Santa Cruz, and Nunnery of St. Clare.—Sir A. Wellesley takes the Command of the Army   24

LETTER VII.

Position of the French.—M. Beresford proceeds to Vizeu with Major-General Tilson's Brigade.—Staff of the Army and Line of Battle - - - - - - - -   28

LETTER VIII.

First movements of the British. Arrival of the Guards at Villanova da Porto.—Passage of the Douro.—Oporto taken and Retreat of the French Army   -   -   -   -   -   35

LETTER IX.

Pursuit of the Enemy to the Borders of Gallicia.—Affair of Salamonde.—Conduct of the Peasantry   -   -   -   -   44

LETTER X.

Return to Oporto.—City of Braga.—Cruelty of the French on their Entrance into Oporto.—Traits of National Character   -   -   -   -   -   -   -   -   -   -   50

LETTER XI.

March of the British to the South of Portugal.—Monastery of Grijon, Pinheiro, Albegaria Velha, and Adega. Halt at Coimbra.   -   -   -   -   -   -   -   55

LETTER XII.

Through Condiexa and Pombal to Leyria Ourem.—City of Thomar.—Arrive at Punhete.—Reflections on the Campaign   57

CONTENTS. vii

LETTER XIII. *Page*

Advance of the British into Spain.—The Guards march to Castel Branco, through Abrantes, Cortiçada, Sobriera Formosa, and Sazedas - - - - - - 62

LETTER XIV.

The British enter Spain at Zarza Major, and arrive at Placentia, where the whole of the Army is concentrated - 66

LETTER XV.

The British form a Junction with Cuesta's Army, and arrive at Talavera de la Reyna.—Position of the French, and Plan of the intended Attack - - - - - - 72

LETTER XVI.

The Combined Army moves from the Wood of Olives, to the Banks of the Alberche.—Retreat of Marshal Victor.—British Out-posts at Caselegas.—The Spaniards occupy Santa Olalla. - - - - - - - 78

LETTER XVII.

Battle of Talavera.—Positions of the Respective Armies. The Enemy foiled in his repeated Attempts to turn the left of the British makes a Grand Attack upon the right and centre.—General Sherbrooke's Division advances to the charge with bayonets.—The Brigade of Guards having advanced too far under a heavy fire, sustain a considerable loss, and retire, covered by the first battalion of the 48th Regiment.—The French retreat during the night.—On the following morning General Robert Crawford's Brigade of Light Infantry arrived - - - - - - - 83

CONTENTS.

LETTER XVIII.

Information received from a French Officer taken prisoner.—Report of Marshal Soult advancing on Placentia - - - - - - - - - 94

LETTER XIX.

Retreat of the Combined Army, to the South Bank of the Tagus.—Particulars of the March.—Cuesta resigns his Command.—The British Prisoners of War treated with great humanity by Marshal Mortier - - - - 99

LETTER XX.

Truxillo.—Tomb of Pizarro, &c. - - - - - 108

LETTER XXI.

Route of the British to Merida.—Short account of the Roman Antiquities in that City - - - - - 110

LETTER XXII.

The 1st division of the British encamp on the Banks of the Guadiana.—Positions of the French - - - 116

LETTER XXIII.

The Guards go into Cantonments in Badajos.—Lieutenant-General Sherbrooke receives the Order of the Bath.—Viscount Wellington's Gala - - - - - - 119

LETTER XXIV.

Birth-day of Ferdinand VII.—The public Promenade of Badajos.—Tertullia.—Remarks.—Situation of the French Corps - - - - - - - - - 121

CONTENTS.

LETTER XXV.

Escape of two British Officers from Madrid, &c. - - 126

LETTER XXVI.

Remarks on some of the leading features of the Campaign.—In consequence of the Army of La Mancha under General Arriesaga being defeated, the British break up from Spain.—Route of the 1st Division.—The Guards at the Head of the Column reach Abrantes, passing through the following places on their march:—Elvas, Barbacena, Montforte, Portalegre, Gafete and Gavio.—Sick left at Abrantes - 128

LETTER XXVII.

March of the Guards to Leyria, &c.   -   - 140

LETTER XXVIII.

The Guards arrive at Vizeu.—Short Account of that ancient City. - - - - - - - - - 142

LETTER XXIX.

The British Army in Winter Quarters.—Marshal Ney summons Ciudad Rodrigo, and Victor overrunning the Province of Andalusia suddenly appears before Cadiz, to which place the Honourable General W. Stewart was dispatched from Lisbon, with a Brigade of Infantry.—Skirmish at the Out-posts - - - - - - - - 149

LETTER XXX.

Description of the Country round Vizeu.—Festival of St. Josephine - - - - - - - 154

CONTENTS.

LETTER XXXI.

Situation of the French Corps—Remarks on the War in the Peninsula.—General Robert Crawford throws himself into Fort Conception - - - - - - - - 157

LETTER XXXII.

The French are making Preparations for the Siege of Ciudad Rodrigo, &c. - - - - - - - 160

LETTER XXXIII.

The British move up to the frontiers.—Head-quarters at Celerico.—Marshal Beresford at Fornos.—Astorga surrenders to Junot.—Massena arrives at Salamanca.—City of Guarda 168

LETTER XXXIV.

Ciudad Rodrigo besieged and taken after a most gallant defence.—The British out-posts withdrawn to Val de Lamula, &c. - . - - . - - - - 169

LETTER XXXV.

General Crawford retires over the Coa, after a smart affair with a greatly superior force of the Enemy.—General Hill's Division crosses the Tagus.—Regnier arrives at Castel Branco.—Movements of the British.—A party of Officers visit the Estrella - - - . - - - - 172

LETTER XXXVI.

Almeida taken, and Retreat of the British - . - 179

LETTER XXXVII.

The combined Army takes up a position on the right Bank of the Mondego.—Battle of Busaco. - - - - 183

CONTENTS

LETTER XXXVIII.

The Combined Army retires to the entrenched Position, in the vicinity of Lisbon, &c. - - - - - 195

LETTER XXXIX.

Retreat of the French.—The British in pursuit, arrive before Santarem, where General R. Crawford is left to watch the Enemy, &c. - - - - 205

LETTER XL.

The French after retiring from before the fortified position in the vicinity of the Capital, are cantoned during the Winter Months in Santarem, Thomar, &c.—Death of the Marquis of Romana.—Sketch of his Character, &c. - - - 213

LETTER XLI.

Retreat of Massena from Santarem, and advance of the British.—Operations during the Pursuit, which is continued until the whole of the Army of Portugal cross the Agueda, leaving Almeida to its fate.—French barbarity - - 221

LETTER XLII.

Massena having collected the whole of the Troops in the North of Spain, makes an attempt to relieve Almeida.—Battle of Fuentes de Honor.—Almeida abandoned by the Garrison - - - - - - - - 242

LETTER XLIII.

Operations of Marshal Sir William Beresford on the Guadiana.—Battle of Albuera.—General Lumley's brilliant Affair with the French Cavalry at Usagre.—The Siege of Badajos raised a second time.—The whole of the Allied Army in

Page

the Alentejo.—Lord Wellington in the beginning of August, recrosses the Tagus, and invests Ciudad Rodrigo, into which, Marmont throws supplies on the 24th of September, and advances over the Aqueda.—The Allied Army takes up a Position in Front of the Coa—Marmont retires - 252

LETTER XLIV.

General remarks on the successful Campaign of 1811.—Observations respecting the Spanish Guerillas, &c. - - 195

ERRATA.

Letter 1, *date, for* 1810 *read* 1809
Page 4, *line* 10, *for* Lion *read* Leon
4, *line* 13, *for* Modina *read* Medina
4, *line* 25, *for* in *read* at
5, *line* 1, *for* our *read* one
6, *lines* 24, 25, *for* westword *read* westward.
11, *line* 10, *for* 200 *read* 300
14, *line* 4, *for* received *read* reviewed
22, *line* 17, *for* stands *read* stand
29, *line* 19, *for* the river *read* that river
30, *line* 2, *for* the *read* a
36, *line* 8, *for* while *read* whilst
53, *line* 21, *for* natural *read* mutual
66, *line* 12, *for* contrived *read* continued
70, *line* 22, *for* century *read* quarter of a
72, *line* 5, (after) where *read* there
73, *line* 4, *for* place *read* plan
79, *line* 24, *for* rear *read* river
136, *line* 8, *for* the time *read* this time
228, *line* 20, *for* burning *read* burying
245, *line* 15, *for* columns *read* column
268, *line* 2, *for* toal *read* total.
271, *line* 15, *for* pretty *read* petty.

A NARRATIVE,

&c. &c.

LETTER I.

The Expedition sails from Portsmouth.—Separated in a Gale of Wind; reassembles at Cork.—Refused Permission to disembark at Cadiz.—Arrival in the Tagus.

On Board the Queen Transport,
Off Lisbon, March 12, 1819.

THE Expedition embarked at Spithead, under the orders of Major-General Sherbrooke, which had been detained for some days by contrary winds, sailed per signal in a fresh gale at N.E. about noon, on Sunday, the 15th of January, 1809, under the protection of the Niobe frigate and Isis of 50 guns.—At 4 P.M. the fleet anchored for the night in Cowes Roads; and at day-break on the following morning, weighed and stood through the Needles with a leading wind.—The masters of the transports went on board the

Niobe for instructions at noon; when they were informed, that the object of the expedition being of the greatest national importance, all possible sail was constantly to be carried during the day. Before dusk, the fleet was off Portland. Next day, while standing down Channel, the Niobe made the signal for Cadiz.

From this time the convoy met with baffling winds and squally weather until the morning of the 30th, when the whole were dispersed in a tremenduous gale of wind; after which some of the transports bore immediately up for Cork, the appointed rendezvous.

On the 25th of February, the whole of the missing ships having previously joined, the fleet again weighed, and stood out of the Cove with a light and favourable breeze, which at sun-set had carried them nearly out of sight of land.

Nothing particular occurred until the 6th of March; when, continuing the voyage with a moderate gale, and fair weather, at 9 A. M. the Niobe telegraphed a large frigate passing through the fleet, and shortly afterwards made the signal for seeing the land,—the rock of Lisbon on the weather bow; and for each ship to pass within hail. Spoke the Commodore, who desired a good look-out to be kept, as the French fleet was at sea, having sailed from Brest on the 3d instant. A British squadron had been detached in pursuit.—At noon the rock of Lisbon bore east 4 or 5 leagues: Cape Espichel S. E. 10 or 12 leagues; steering due south.

By some mismanagement, the PrinceGeorge transport, the head quarters ship of the Coldstream Guards fell on board His Majesty's ship Isis about 11 o'clock at night. In the alarm naturally occasioned by such an event, occurring too at so late an hour, from which the most fatal consequences were to be apprehended, several of the officers and men jumped on board the Isis; but Ensign Long failed in the attempt, and was unfortunately drowned. The transport soon after got clear of His Majesty's ship, with the loss of her mizen-mast.

At midnight the fleet hauled round Cape St. Vincent. On the following morning Cape

St. Mary bore N. E. by E. at the distance of 7 or 8 leagues. The Niobe under a press of sail a-head. At 10 P. M. shortened sail, the Commodore having hove to.

At 2 A. M. on the 8th instant saw the lights of Cadiz. At dawn of day the city appeared right a-head, about 5 leagues distant. The fleet ran along the shore, having a beautiful view of the Carraccas, the Isle of Lion, and the inner harbour, in which lay the Spanish men of war and the French prizes. In the distance appeared the lofty mountains of Modina Sidonia. A British squadron, one ship bearing the flag of Rear-Admiral Purvis, lay at anchor in the outer harbour.

At half-past 2 P. M. a lugger from the Admiral spoke the Niobe; immediately after which the signal was made to rendezvous in the Tagus. At this time the ships were close in with the city, and the inhabitants were distinctly observed enjoying the sea breeze on the tops of their houses, which are all flat-roofed, in the form of a terrace.

Cadiz, seated in the extremity of a peninsula, appeared a well-built handsome city, with several magnificent edifices.—Our great necessary of life is wanting; namely, fresh water, which is brought in boats at a considerable expense across the bay from Port St. Mary's. The harbour is formed by Fort St. Sebastian on the south, and the town of Rota on the north. The entrance is strongly fortified; and, indeed, every assailable point is protected by heavy batteries.—The river Guadalette, the fabled Lethé of the ancients, falls into the bay of Cadiz.

The master of a transport which had entered the harbour, and was boarded by a boat from the British fleet, was informed that a division of troops, under the command of Major-General Mackenzie, after remaining at Cadiz for upwards of a month, without being permitted to land, sailed on the preceding day for Lisbon. This intelligence occasioned various surmises; as the conduct of the Spaniards, in refusing to admit an English force into Cadiz, could not be reconciled with what had been previously and industriously proclaimed respecting the disposition of this nation towards Great Britain.

The wind continuing favourable, at day-light yesterday the fleet arrived off the mouth of the Tagus. About 8 o'clock, the Portugueze pilots came on board, and took charge of the ships. Nothing can be conceived more delightful than the view of Lisbon in sailing up the river. The day was remarkably fine; and, as the fleet advanced, every object, so late in possession of the enemy, forcibly engaged the attention of the British troops. At the bottom of the mountain, which is called the Rock of Lisbon, stands the small town of Cascaes; beyond that, the convent of St. Antonio, beautifully situated close to the beach, under the shelter of a fine grove of pines. Half a mile to the eastward is Fort St. Antonio; and two miles higher up, Fort St. Julian; which, in conjunction with the Bugio, a circular battery of two tiers of cannon on the opposite side of the channel, protects the entrance of the Tagus, and certainly presents a most formidable obstacle to the passage of a hostile fleet. About two leagues above Fort St. Julian, stands the ancient Moorish Castle of Belem; to the westword of which, and immediately adjoining, a large half-moon battery has recently been constructed. Several smaller forts line the north bank of the river, but the whole are commanded by superior eminences, consequently untenable on the land side. At 5 P.M. the fleet anchored a little above Belem Castle, and opposite to the convent, one of the few edifices of note which were not overthrown in the memorable earthquake of 1755, at which time nearly the whole of Lisbon was destroyed. On this melancholy occasion several thousands of the wretched inhabitants sought shelter, and were received within its consecrated walls. This noble Gothic pile was erected on the spot where the daring Vasco de Gama received the benediction of the Patriarch of Lisbon, before he embarked on his voyage of discovery.

LETTER II.

Short Account of Lisbon.—The Churches, Aqueduct, &c.—
Reported Situation of the French Armies, under Marshals
Soult and Victor.

Lisbon, March 16, 1809.

MAJOR-GENERAL SHERBROOKE having previously issued orders, that the troops should adopt a conciliating mode of conduct towards the Portuguese nation in general, and pay particular respect to the religious ceremonies of the country; on the morning of the 13th instant, his division disembarked.

The second brigade of Guards, under the command of Brigadier-General H. F. Campbell, occupied the barracks at Belem. The officers were quartered upon the inhabitants, who in general evinced the utmost civility and attention to their accommodation. Major-General Tilson's brigade, consisting of the 2d batallion of the 87th regiment, and 1st of the 88th, was quartered in Lisbon, and formed the garrison of the capital.

Lisbon is adorned with several handsome streets and squares, particularly the Real

Praça de Commercio, where is an equestrian statue in bronze of Joseph the 1st.; but the general appearance of this metropolis cannot fail to disgust a stranger, owing to the extreme filth which meets the eye in every part, and is unpardonable, as its situation on the banks of a noble river, from which Lisbon derives more important commercial advantages than any other capital in Europe, London excepted, affords the utmost facility for keeping the streets perfectly clean.

The city is of great extent, reaching from below Belem, to which it is joined by a continuation of buildings to Marivala, along the beach, a distance of nearly seven miles, but the breadth is irregular, owing to the high grounds which rise up in almost every direction from the banks of the Tagus. The principal street is called the Rua Augusta, adjoining the grand square of the Roscio, in which the Palace of the Inquisition, now occupied by the Regency, is situated. Near this are the theatres of the Salitre and Rua das Condes. There are no public buildings of sufficient consequence to merit attention, excepting the churches, the generality of which are decorated in a most splendid style. And although it may be from motives of policy that so much splendour is exhibited in their religious edifices, as it must have a powerful effect on the minds of the ignorant and bigotted, yet to adorn the temples of God with all possible magnificence, seems to be but paying a proper homage to the Deity.

The Estrella convent, which was built by the present Queen, and the churches of St. Domingo, St. Francis, and St. Roque, are pointed out to strangers as particularly deserving of notice. In the latter is the celebrated chapel of St. John the Baptist, made entirely at Rome, by order of King John the Fifth, of exquisite workmanship, and embellished with the most beautiful paintings, in mosaic. The frontispiece of silver chased ornaments, had been taken down, and packed up to send to Paris, by order of Junôt.

Excepting the old castle, Lisbon has no other means of defence; works however, might be erected on the hills, forming the environs of the city, which would considerably retard the approach of a hostile army, but nothing of the kind has as yet been attempted.

At a short distance from the city, is the noble Aqueduct thrown across the vale of Alcantara, which supplies the whole of Lisbon with the waters of the Pusilippo. This princely specimen of modern architecture is above a mile in length, and is supported on seventy fine grand arches, the centre and principal one being upwards of 200 feet in height, from the bed of a small river which runs under it. Its amazing strength enabled it to resist the effects of the great earthquake on the 1st of November, 1755.

There are several good taverns in Lisbon; the Golden Lion, La Tour's, Barnwell's, charmingly situated at Buenos Ayres, &c.

This being Lent, the theatres and opera are shut, which is the less to be regretted, particularly the opera, as since the departure of Catalani, Vestris, and Angiolini, the Italian theatre no longer enjoys its former reputation.

At Belem are the royal gardens, which, although magnificent, are in too formal a style to please an English taste. A few rare birds remain in the aviary, but the menagerie was completely emptied by Junôt.

The royal museum still contains a great number of natural curiosities, although a considerable quantity had been carried off by the French, and many rare productions wantonly destroyed.

Among other objects of attraction in the beautiful environs of Lisbon, is the palace of Queluz, a league from the capital, on the road to Cintra, which place, from the salubrity of its air, is esteemed the Montpelier of Portugal. The surrounding country, comprising the rugged mountain, with the convent of Pina, is highly picturesque, and the blue waves of the Atlantic ocean, terminating the prospect on the west, impart a character of sublimity and grandeur to the varied and romantic scenery.

Two leagues from hence, and seven from Lisbon, stands the abbey of Mafra, celebrated for its fine gardens and extensive library. Here the court were accustomed annually to spend a few weeks in solitude. One league beyond, is Torres Vedras, the Turres Veteres of the Romans.

A stranger is particularly struck by the apparent devotion of the people in the streets, who on hearing a bell announce the approach of the host, drop on their knees, and remain in that position, however unfavourable the weather, saying their prayers and crossing themselves until it has passed. The several town guards are turned out and present arms, and the officers and soldiers of the British army, halt and take off their hats, in conformity with the orders issued to that effect.

At present little is known here respecting the movements of the French, except that they threaten the northern and eastern frontiers of the kingdom. The Portuguese seem to be in a state of apathy, and are apparently taking no measures for the defence of their country; but it is to be hoped, they will be roused from this inactivity should the enemy actually make an irruption into Portugal.

LETTER III.

The Guards march to Saccavem.—Sir John Craddock moves his Head Quarters to Lumiar.—Account received of Marshal Soult having taken Oporto.—Marshal Beresford sets out for Thomar.

Saccavem, March 30, 1809.

A PARTIAL change has taken place in the quarters of the army.

On the 18th instant, the guards marched into Lisbon, and were received by Lieut. General Sir John Craddock, commander of the forces. Two days afterwards the brigade commenced its route along the north bank of the Tagus. The Coldstream occupied the town of Saccavem, and the 3d regiment halted about noon at Olivias, a small but beautiful village surrounded with groves of olives and vineyards, two miles in the rear.

On the 22d, the 3d guards advanced, and took up a strong position; the town of Saccavem, about a mile to the right, and a small river running through a deep valley in its course to the Tagus, in their immediate front. The left of the battalion extended to the village of Unhos, a distance of two miles. The walks in the vicinity are delightful, and the hedges, in which grow spontaneously the Indian fig, the myrtle, and the orange, impart a most grateful fragrance to the air.

The commander of the forces has removed his head quarters to Lumiar, and the several brigades of infantry are drawn in a cordon round the capital; the left of the whole being at Alcantara.

General Beresford, who has been honoured with the rank of marshal, by the Regency, is about to proceed with a numerous staff to Thomar, in order to organize the new levies assembling in that city.

The intelligence of M. Soult, with an army of twenty-four thousand men having taken Oporto, creates a considerable sensation. A number of the inhabitants of that city and neighbourhood, on hearing the approach of the enemy, quitted it, and have arrived in Lisbon. Among others, the venerable Archbishop of Braga and suite. The reports of the enormities committed by the French on gaining possession of Oporto, almost exceed belief; but they are unhappily too well authenticated.

Every exertion is making in the several departments to enable the army to commence active operations. In a few days it is expected the troops will leave their present position, and take up another in advance.

LETTER IV.

Continue their March through Alhandra, Carregada and Alcoentre, to Riomayor.—Description of the Country on the Route.

Riomayor, April 17, 1809.

THE campaign may now be said to have commenced, and thus far have the British advanced into the heart of Portugal.

On the morning of the 9th instant, the army was put in motion. The brigade of Guards marched to Alhandra, three Portuguese leagues or twelve miles, and arrived about one o'clock. The baggage was carried on mules, no wheel-carriages being allowed in the line of march but to general officers. Alhandra is delightfully situated at the base of a range of hills cloathed with vineyards.

On the following day the Guards resumed their march about nine o'clock, and soon after mid-day went into cantonments. The Coldstream and light infantry at Villa Nova da Rainha, the 3d regiment at Carregada. The route was through the towns of Villa Franca da Xira and Castanheira, situated on the banks of the Tagus.

Next day, General Alexander Campbell's brigade consisting of the second battalions of the 7th and 53d regiments arrived at Castanheira.

After a halt of three days, the division advanced at day-break on the 14th to Alcaentre, a small town, nearly four leagues from Carregada. Soon after leaving the latter place, the smiling fertile plains of Lower Estremadura were succeeded by a bleak and partially cultivated district, where nothing relieved the eye for many miles but a few scattered cork and pine trees. In some parts of this dreary region wooden crosses were erected to mark the spot where murder had been committed, and these sad memorials of human depravity are but too frequent throughout this kingdom.

The dust on this day's march was particularly troublesome. At one the brigade halted. Part of the 3d regiment was quartered in the Chateau of the Condé de Lumiar, a large and once magnificent pile, but now abandoned to the care of a few domestics, and scarcely habitable. The grounds, although quite neglected, are still beautiful; and the situation of the castle embosomed in trees, was rendered peculiarly striking from its bursting unexpectedly upon the view, after a long march over a sandy tract of country.

The next morning at daylight the Guards proceeded on their route, and at the end of three leagues reached this place. The country at first bore a similar feature to that through which they had marched the preceding day, when within a league of the town the road led through a deep and extensive forest of pines intermixed with the olive.

General Alexander Campbell's brigade marched into quarters here about an hour afterwards.

Riomayor is an inconsiderable town on the banks of a small river, which, taking a southerly direction falls into the Tagus below Santarem.

At the distance of three miles is a cavern in a romantic glen, in which several families had taken refuge on the first entrance of the French into Portugal. There is nothing remarkable in the appearance of the cavern, but the surrounding scenery is inexpressibly beautiful, and adorned by some very fine cork trees, several of which measured upwards of twenty feet in circumference.

Sir John Craddock with the principal part of the army has arrived at Caldas, five leagues on the left.

LETTER V.

Convent of St. Dominick at Batalha.—Leyria.—Sir John Craddock takes leave of the Army.—Bishop's Palace, &c.

Leyria, April 26, 1809.

AT four on the morning of the 21st instant, the general beat; and exactly at five, the column moved off on the road leading to Oporto. This day's march was long and fatiguing; about seven leagues or twenty-eight miles,—the road one of the best in Portugal, made by order of the Marquis of Pombal. No water was to be procured on the march; but of this the troops had been previously informed. The Guards arrived at Batalha about five o'clock, and nearly the whole were quartered in the ancient Convent of St. Dominick. At six, an excellent dinner was served up to the officers in the refectory: the Prior himself, with several of the monks, attended during the repast. After dinner, they were conducted to see the body of John the Second, which was still in tolerable preservation, although the monarch had been dead upwards of three hundred years. The architecture of the Convent excited universal admiration: a beautiful corridor run round each story; and it is perhaps the most magnificent specimen of the Arabesque remaining in Europe, with the exception of the palace of the Alhambra at Grenada.

Next morning, at an early hour, the officers took leave of the hospitable brethren of St. Dominick; and after a march of two short leagues, the brigade arrived at Leyria about eight o'clock.

This city, seated in a fertile valley, watered by the small river Leyes, is the see of a bishop. Its first appearance is particularly impressive. On a high isolated rock stands the ruins of an old castle, proudly overlooking the city, and forming a remarkable contrast with the bishop's palace, a handsome modern building immediately below. Nearly adjoining is the cathedral, which has nothing striking in its exterior appearance, but is richly decorated within. In the palace are a few pictures, but none of any merit. The principal suite of apartments opened to a terrace, commanding rich and beautiful views of this picturesque country.

Considerable anxiety is now felt respecting the future operations, and a variety of opinions and reports are in circulation. By some, it is supposed, that the army will remain quietly in Leyria, covering the capital; while others conjecture, that it is intended to advance in the course of a few days to attack Marshal Soult in Oporto; although, the situation of Victor's army, on the right flank, but on the opposite side of the Tagus, seems to present an obstacle to a further advance in that direction.

Yesterday, Sir John Craddock set off for Lisbon on his way to Gibraltar, of which fortress he has been appointed Lieutenant-Governor. His Excellency, in general orders, expressed his entire approbation of the conduct of the troops in the trying situation in which they were placed; and his deep regret, at being removed from the command of this gallant army at a crisis of such importance, which it was not in the power of any consideration to alleviate.

LETTER VI.

The Army assembles at Coimbra.—Description of that City.—Camoens.—Monastery of Santa Cruz and Nunnery of St. Clare.—Sir Arthur Wellesley takes the Command of the Army.

Coimbra, May 3, 1809.

THE whole of the army, with the exception of Major-General Mackenzie's brigade, which had been detached to the right, was assembled in Coimbra about the beginning of May.

Soon after morning parade on the 29th of April, a sudden order was issued for the army to advance; and, by noon, the Guards, with General Richard Stewart's brigade, moved off on the road to Oporto in a heavy fall of rain. After a march of four leagues, about seven in the evening the column halted in the town of Pombal, which possessed nothing remarkable but a fine old castle in a commanding situation. Next day, the troops reached Condeixa about two o'clock; distance five leagues.

At day-break, on the 1st of May, the division resumed its march; and soon after mid-day, arrived at Coimbra. From the summit of a hill, on gaining which, the first view is caught of the city, the road led by a winding direction for above a mile through a wood of olives to the bridge over the Mondego; on the northern bank of which Coimbra is situated.—The appearance of the British troops was hailed by the inhabitants with the most lively demonstrations of joy.

This is the seat of learning; for Coimbra contains the only university in Portugal. Here Camoens, the pride and boast of his country, received his education; and on the banks of the Mondego, he first wooed the Muse, and composed several of his most admired sonnets. The vale, through which this river glides, is of great extent and beauty, and might well be supposed to have excited the most sublime ideas in the bosom of the author of the Lusiad. Of his attachment to Coimbra, Camoens gives numerous proofs in his writings. With peculiar delight, the poet frequently recurs to a description of the romantic scenery amidst which in early youth he sought recreation from his literary pursuits.

The several classes are held in the college

of St. Paul's, which had been the Royal residence before the seat of government was removed to Lisbon. The number of students is usually about a thousand; but the whole are at present dispersed, in consequence of the critical situation of the country. A few remained in Coimbra; and about three hundred are formed into an armed association, called the Academic corps, commanded by Lieut.-Colonel Trant.

The library of this College is very extensive, and fitted-up in an elegant style.—From the top of a high tower, to which the ascent is by a narrow winding staircase, a fine view is obtained of the surrounding country, and the course of the Mondego, until it falls into the vast Atlantic.

Yesterday, about two o'clock, the arrival of Sir Arthur Wellesley was announced by the firing of rockets; and the bells of the different churches immediately commenced a peal of joy. Surrounded by a numerous staff, the commander of the forces rode to his quarters amidst the acclamations of the people, who testified the highest delight on beholding the hero of Vimeira. At night, the city was brilliantly illuminated in honour of His Excellency.

The monastery of Santa Cruz, where Head Quarters were established, is inhabited by monks of the rich order of St. Augustine. As a particular favour, the British officers were allowed to see the sanctuary, into which few strangers are ever admitted. Here, the intelligent French Abbé St. Croix, who had emigrated from his native country at an early period of the revolution, had taken refuge.

On the south bank of the Mondego, and immediately opposite to the city, stands the magnificent convent of St. Clare. The nuns, who are of the first families in Portugal, were much pleased with the visits of the British officers at the grate, and sought to amuse them by the spontaneous exertion of their talents in singing and music. Several of them were handsome, and would be thought so even in England. The peculiarity of their dress was certainly unfavourable to the display of their personal charms, and formed a remarkable contrast with the *naïveté* of their manners.

LETTER VII.

Position of the French.—Marshal Beresford proceeds to Vizeu with Major-General Tilson's Brigade.—Staff of the Army and Line of Battle.

Coimbra, May 7, 1809.

THE position of the enemy, against whom it was generally supposed the British were destined to act in the first instance, was understood to be as follows: Marshal Soult with the main-body of his army, is in Oporto; and his advanced guard, composed of cavalry, under the command of General Franceschi, on the north side of the Vouga. The total number of the French is stated at 24,000; but this force is very much scattered at present, as they occupy Viana on the Lima river, and Valence and Tuy on the Minho. The latter is an important post, being the ferry which communicates with Gallicia; and they have moved all the boats on the Minho, as well as those which belong to Viana, to this point.

Victor's army is in the neighbourhood of Badajos, but not advancing. Major General Mackenzie's brigade is stationed at Abrantes;

the Lusitanian legion under Colonel Mayne as a corps of observation at Alcantara; and the principal part of the Portuguese army has been collected in the valley of the Tagus. There are gun boats moored in the river as high up as Azambujo, manned by thorough bred seamen, volunteers from the transports; and this little naval force has some long guns on the shore attached to it. The engineers have ascertained that Lisbon can be bombarded from the opposite heights, for which purpose the enemy may probably move a corps through the Alemtejo on the peninsula betwixt the Tagus and St. Ubes.

Colonel Trant with about two thousand Portuguese is in front on the banks of the Vouga, keeping a vigilant watch on the movements of the French, and Sir Robert Wilson is also on the river, commanding the advanced corps of Brigadier General Barcellar's division of the Portuguese army which is stationed at Vizeu.

Several battalions of Portuguese infantry are already united with the British brigades. Marshal Beresford, who came to Coimbra on the arrival of Sir Arthur Wellesley, moved forward on the morning of the 5th instant, with Major General Tilson, and the division of troops on the road to Lamego. Yesterday Sir Arthur Wellesley reviewed his army on the extensive plain below the city.

The following is a list of the staff of this army, and the order of the line of battle as given out in general orders:

Lieut. Gen. the Rt. H. Sir A. Wellesley, K.B. Commander of the Forces.

Lieut. Col. Bathurst, Military Secretary.

Captains The Hon. Fitzroy Stanhope; Lord Fitzroy Somerset; George Bouverie; and C. F. Canning, Aides de Camp.

Major Generals——Sherbrooke; Payne; Lord William Bentinck; and the Honorable E. Paget, with the local rank of Lieutenant Generals during the continuance of this service.

Major Generals—Cotton; Hill; Murray; Erskine; Mackenzie, and Tilson.

Brigadier Generals—A. Campbell; H. F. Campbell; R. Stewart; Cameron; Fane; Drieberg; and Langworth.

Colonel Donkin, Colonel on the Staff.

Adjutant Generals' Department.
Brigadier General the Hon. C. Stewart; Adjutant General, Lieut. Colonels Darrock, 36 regiment; Lord Aylmer, Coldstream; Edwards, Heimber, 68th regiment; Elley, Horse Guards; Majors Tidy, 14th regiment; Williamson, 30th; Berkeley, and C. Campbell.

Assistant Adjutant Generals.
Captains Cotton; Elliot; Dashwood; Graham; Cockburn; Mellish; and During,
Deputy Assistant Adjutant Generals.

Quarter-Master Generals' Department.
Col. Murray, 3d Guards, Quart. Mast. Gen.
Lieut. Col. Delancey, Dep. Quart. Mast. Gen.

Lieutenant Colonels Bathurst; Bourke;
Majors Blaquiere and Northey,
Assistant Quarter-Master Generals.

Captains Mercer; Sutton; Langton; Kelly; Heverfield; Scovil; Waller; and Beresford;
Deputy Assistant Quarter-Master Generals.

The army is brigaded, and will stand in line as follows : viz.

CAVALRY.

Lieut. Gen. Payne and Major-Gen. Cotton.

14th Light Dragoons   Colonel Hawker.
20th   ditto   Major Blake.
3d K.'s Ger. Lt. Hussars   Lt.Col.Arentschild.
16th Light Dragoons   Colonel Anson.

GUARDS.

Brigadier General H. F. Campbell.

1st Battalion Coldstream   Lieut. Col. Hulse.
1st Battal. 3d Regiment   Hon.Col.Stopford.
1st Company 60th   Captain Haines.

INFANTRY.

1st Brigade, Major-General Hill.

3d or Buffs   Lieut. Col. Muter.
66th Reg. 2d Bat.   Major Murray.
48th ditto   Lieut. Col. Duckworth.
60th 1st Company

3d Brigade, Major-General Tilson.

60th 5 companies   Major Woodgate.

88th 1st Battalion   Major Vandeleur.
1st Battalion Portuguese Grenadiers.
87th 2d Battalion   Major Gough.

5th Brigade, Brigadier-General A. Campbell.

7th 2d Battalion   Lieut. Col. Sir W. Myers.
53d ditto   Lieut. Col. Bingham.
16th Portuguese, 1st Bat.   Lieut. Col. Oliver.
60th 1 Company.

7th Brigade, Brigadier-General Cameron.

9th Regiment   Lieutenant-Colonel Molle.
10th Portuguese, 2d Battalion.
83d Regiment, ditto   Lieut. Col. Gordon.
60th 1 Company.

6th Brigade, Brigadier-General R. Stewart.

*Detachments 1st Batal.   Lieut. Col. Bunbury.
16th Portuguese Regiment   Lieut. Col. Doyle.
29th Regiment   Lieut. Col. White.

4th Brigade, Brigadier-General Sontag.

*Detachments 2d Battal.   Lieut. Col. Copson.
16th Portuguese.

---

* The Battalions of Detachments were formed of those soldiers of Sir John Moore's army who were left sick in Lisbon, or fell out from sickness in the march through Portugal to Salamanca, and the sick and stragglers during the retreat to Corunna.

97th Regiment   Lieut. Col. Lyon.
60th 1 Company.

   2d Brigade, Major-General Mackenzie.
27th Regiment, 3d Bat.   Lieut. Col. Maclean.
45th   ditto   1st   Lieut. Col. Guard.
31st   ditto   2d   Major Watson.

KING'S GERMAN LEGION.
Major-General Murray,
WITH
Brigadier-Generals Drieberg and Langworth.

ROYAL ARTILLERY.
Brigadier-General Howarth.
Lieut. Colonels Framlingham and Robe.

LETTER VIII.

First Movements of the British.—Arrival of the Guards at Villa Nova da Porto.—Passage of the Douro.—Oporto taken, and Retreat of the French Army.

Oporto, May 13, 1811.

AFTER a series of operations, conducted with the utmost rapidity and attended with the happiest success, terminated by an atchievement second to none recorded in the page of history, either for boldness of conception or the promptitude with which it was carried into execution,—Sir Arthur Wellesley, on the 12th of May, obtained possession of this important city.

The following is a detail of the movements of the British from the hour of their leaving Coimbra, until the auspicious moment, when Lieutenant-General Paget, with a handful of men, made good the passage of the Douro in the face of a formidable enemy.

On the morning of the 8th instant, Lieutenant-General Payne, with the brigades of cavalry and infantry, under the command of

Major-Generals Cotton and Hill, marched from Coimbra, the latter by way of Aviero, at which place the infantry was to embark for Ovar, and turn the enemy's right by the road on the sea-coast.

The first and immediate object of the commander in chief, was to dispossess the enemy of Oporto; and while the principal force was employed in the attack upon the main body of the French in that city, Marshal Beresford was directed to proceed with his division by Lamego on the Upper Douro, and cross the river at that point, for the purpose of diverting the enemy's attention.

On the following day, the brigade of Guards, with those of Brigadier-Generals Sontag, A. Campbell, and Cameron, advanced from Coimbra with the whole of the artillery and stores attached to them. Brigadier-General Cameron took the road of Aviero; the Guards halted about three o'clock at Familicoa, and the other two brigades occupied Malheada and adjacent villages in the rear.

May the 10th.—The march of the troops was resumed at day-light; and, at two o'clock, the head of the column arrived upon the bridge over the Vouga. Generals Payne and Cotton with the cavalry, and Colonel Trant with the Portuguese under his command, had passed the river late on the preceding evening, and early this morning drove in the advanced posts of the enemy; who, after making a short resistance, retreated on the road to Oporto pursued by the British. The Honourable Major Lincoln Stanhope was wounded in the arm by a sabre in charging the enemy with a squadron of his regiment, the 16th Light Dragoons. At six o'clock, the Guards halted in the miserable village of Albegaria Nova, where the French had converted the dwellings of the inhabitants into stables.

May the 11th.—Much depending on the rapidity of movement, the Guards were again under arms at an early hour; and having halted to refresh themselves from ten o'clock until noon in the small town of Penhieros, about five in the evening they arrived at St. Antonia de Arifana, the head quarters of the reserve for the night,—twenty-four miles from Oporto. The pursuit of the enemy had been continued by General Payne to a position, the heights of Grigon, about three leagues from that city, whence a reinforcement was sent by Marshal Soult, making their numbers amount to nearly five thousand men. Upon this body a spirited attack was made by Brigadier-General R. Stewart, and Major-General Murray, by a well conducted movement with a brigade of the King's German Legion, turned the left flank of the enemy; who, in retreating, was charged by two squadrons of the 16th and 20th Dragoons under Major Blake, led on by Brigadier-General the Honourable C. Stewart, assisted by Lieutenant-Colonel Delancey, Captain Mellish, and Captain Dashwood. The advance of the British took up a position on the hill beyond Carvalhos, within two short leagues of Oporto.

The brigade of Generals A. Campbell and Sontag, which halted yesterday in Albeguria Velha, were this evening quartered in Penheiros.

The faintest tints of dawn appeared in the horizon as the Guards quitted their cantonments yesterday to advance. The intelligence of the preceding evening had led the troops to expect an immediate meeting with the enemy; but it was now learnt that he had retired with considerable precipitation during the night, and destroyed the bridge of boats across the Douro. The troops continued to advance, and entered Villa Nova da Porto about two o'clock, when they had the satisfacfaction of finding that a part of the army had already crossed the river in boats, assisted by the Portuguese, notwithstanding the vigilance of the French sentries, and were at that moment engaged with the enemy.

From the Sierra Convent, situated on the south bank of the Douro, the Commander of the forces had observed the French retiring to a height immediately above the city, and, with the intention of cutting off their rear-guard, he pushed three companies of the Buffs across the river, under Lieutenant-General Paget, who was directed, in the event of being pressed, to throw himself into a convent, which the enemy could not approach without being exposed to a destructive fire from some guns advantageously placed in the gardens of the convent. The result happened as Sir Arthur Wellesley had foreseen. The enemy's columns, on observing the movements of the British, descended from the height to re-enter

Oporto; but by this time Major-General Hill had crossed the Douro with his brigade, which he was enabled to effect with great celerity by the unremitting and voluntary exertions of the Portuguese in navigating the boats. Nearly at the same moment a squadron of the 14th Light Dragoons, under Major Hervey, and two pieces of artillery, were got over, and Major-General Murray, who had passed the river, a few miles above, with a battalion of the King's German Legion, appeared on the left flank of the enemy, who found himself compelled to retire, but took up a more advantageous position, where he seemed determined to make a stand. The Guards now received orders to advance, and were embarked as they reached the Douro, under the superintendance of Colonel Donkin, with the most perfect regularity. Although harrassed by a fatiguing march of upwards of eighty miles in four days, over a most difficult country, yet no sooner were they formed on the opposite shore, than the whole began to run up the steep streets of Oporto, and continued their exertions until the head of the column was ordered to halt. In passing along, the brigade was cheered with repeated shouts of *Viva Inglezes*, by the inhabitants, who hailed the British as their deliverers. The smiles of the young ladies at the balconies, their white handkerchiefs waving as the troops approached, and the prayers of the aged, accompanied with tears, for their success, formed a most interesting scene. The way was somewhat obstructed by the artillery and waggons of ammunition which the enemy had abandoned in his retreat. Amid these lay the bodies of the dead and wounded Frenchmen, already stripped by the Portuguese, and exhibiting a most painful sight.

The brigade had only halted a few minutes, when a considerable number of prisoners, chiefly wounded, were brought in, and the enemy, who at first made a shew of maintaining his position, finding himself pressed on both flanks, retired in great confusion, after a spirited charge of the 14th Dragoons by Major Hervey, towards the hill of Valongo, about a league in front. There the commander of the forces determined on leaving him for the night, satisfied with the advantages he had already obtained. The French must have suffered considerably in the action, but on the side of the British the loss was trifling, compared with the importance of the victory they had gained, which in less than three hours had given them possession of Oporto, the second city in the kingdom.

After remaining a short time on the ground, the British marched into quarters, and were received by the inhabitants in the most hospitable manner.

Marshal Soult was completely surprised in Oporto, and consequently had made no arrangements for the removal of his sick, of whom above a thousand were found in the hospitals. It certainly was in his contemplation to evacuate Portugal, his army having been considerably diminished by sickness; but this he meant to put in execution at his leisure, conceiving himself perfectly secure by the destruction of the bridge; and Loison had been detached towards Amarante to oppose the progress of Marshal Beresford in that direction. Nothing could exceed the astonishment and distress of the French Chief, on being assured that the British were actually crossing the Douro, and this bold movement was equally unexpected on the part of the Portuguese.

The conduct of Marshal Soult must be considered as the best eulogium on the merits of this enterprise, as he is universally acknowledged to be one of the best officers in Bonaparte's service, and as such, is said to enjoy a considerable portion of his master's esteem.

LETTER IX.

Pursuit of the Enemy to the Borders of Galicia.—Affair of Salamondé.—Conduct of the Peasantry.

Travessa, on the Northern Frontier of Portugal,
May 19, 1809.

THE exertions of the army for several days succeeding the capture of Oporto, were unremitting, and of the most fatiguing description.

The bridge over the Davé having been repaired, on the 14th instant the 16th Light Dragoons, the brigade of Guards, and Brigadier-General Cameron's, advanced to Villa Nova de Familicoa, on the road to Braga, with the intention of cutting off Marshal Soult's retreat by that direction into Spain. On the march it was understood that the commander of the forces had received information from Marshal Beresford, of his having defeated General Loison, near the bridge of Amaranté, and that he was pursuing the fugitives towards Chaves.

Next day the column reached Braga about

noon. Marshal Soult had taken up a position at the distance of a league and a half, and was supposed to meditate an attempt at pushing through the city in the night, with a view of getting into the road to Tuy and Valence. About two in the morning, the French drove in the out piquets; but this was merely a feint, as immediately afterwards they continued their route towards the frontiers. At four the column marched; and although the rain on this and the two preceding days was nearly incessant, yet the spriits of the troops were kept up by the hope of overtaking the flying foe. This hope was partly verified; for about six in the evening the enemy was discovered by the advance, posted in the village and adjacent heights of Salamondé. Lieutenant-Colonel Fuller of the Coldstream Guards, commenced the attack with the Light Infantry of the brigade, which would have been followed up by the whole division; but on the approach of night the French fled, after sustaining a trifling loss. As it continued to rain during the night, and no cover could be obtained, the troops were in a most uncomfortable situation, only to be equalled by that of the defeated enemy. Next morning (the 17th) several prisoners were taken in the woods, and a considerable quantity of baggage was found. It was now discovered that the French had been enabled to retire by the left, over a small bridge, which only admitted the passage of one at a time. The armed peasantry had been directed to oppose the enemy at this point, but, unfortunately, some Swiss troops, cloathed in red, under the command of General Reynaud, being mistaken for British, were permitted to cross, and by the dispersion of the Portuguese, the remains of the rear-guard were enabled to effect their escape, but many fell over the precipices in the darkness of the night, and were drowned in the river Cavedo, which was considerably swelled by the late rains.

About noon the column moved forward, and at dusk halted in the village of Ruvaens, without seeing any thing of the enemy. This place afforded very indifferent accommodation, and there was no possibility of bringing forward wine for the troops, the advance being much too rapid, and the roads so bad as to preclude the carriage over this mountainous district.

On the 18th the army marched at daybreak, and in the course of a few hours the British found themselves again in the track of the enemy, who had burnt several villages in his retreat. A number of men and horses lay dead in the roads, as the French destroyed all the animals who, from weakness, were unable to proceed, to prevent them from falling into the hands of the British. At three in the afternoon the column, consisting of a brigade of Artillery, the 16th Light Dragoons, the Guards, a brigade of the King's German Legion, and Brigadier-General Cameron's, was halted for about an hour within two leagues of Montalegre, the frontier town of Portugal. The several corps were then cantoned in the adjoining villages, which they found deserted by the inhabitants. Strong parties of French cavalry had visited them in the morning, and carried off all the bread and wine they could find.

This morning the British remained in their quarters, it being ascertained that M. Soult had entered Gallicia with the remains of his army. Major-General J. Murray, with his Aid-de-Camp, witnessed the retreat of the enemy from Montalegre; his columns marched slowly, and appeared to be in great distress.

It must ever be regretted, that the British were not enabled to advance immediately after the action on the 12th at Oporto; when the enemy, dispirited by his defeat, and astonished at the boldness of Sir Arthur Wellesley's measures, might have been alarmed into an unconditional surrender. But it was found impossible to move the army forward without supplies of every description, the rapidity of the advance from Coimbra having outstripped the most active exertions of the Commissariat, and the country through which the troops were destined to pursue the French, not affording the means of subsistence. Owing to these circumstances, and the want of precision in the execution of some important orders issued by the commander of the forces, Marshal Soult, although surrounded with difficulties of no ordinary nature, had the good fortune to accomplish his escape; but his division may be considered as completely *hors de combat* for the present, and he has lost the whol of his artillery and baggage.

In reviewing the events of this short, but most active campaign, it is impossible not to feel considerable mortification, that the vigorous and well concerted measures, which were adopted for the total annihilation of the enemy, did not experience a more prosperous result.

The behaviour of the Portuguese, who accompanied the British in the pursuit of the enemy, was the natural consequence of the vengeance and deadly hatred, excited in their bosoms by the barbarous excesses which the French had committed; armed with any sort of weapons they could pick up, the peasantry hung upon the rear and flanks of the retreating enemy, and put to death every straggler from the main body, who was not so fortunate as to be saved by the advanced guard. The French have eventually suffered for the cruelty of their conduct; every information respecting the movements of the British troops having been carefully withheld from their knowledge, by the exasperated Portuguese.

LETTER X.

Return to Oporto.—City of Braga.—Cruelty of the French, on their entrance into Oporto.—Traits of national character.

Oporto, 27*th May,* 1809.

The British commenced their descent from the mountains, on the 20th of May, and in the afternoon of the 24th, re-entered Oporto. The weather as they returned to the south, became daily more mild and favorable; and in the prospect of getting into comfortable quarters, the troops seemed to forget their recent hardships and privations.

The Alpine scenery of the inhospitable region bordering upon Gallicia and the Tralos Montes, bore a strong resemblance, in many places, to the Highlands of Scotland, but on approaching the environs of Braga, the face of the country assumed a very different appearance. At the distance of 8 or 9 miles from the city, on the high isolated rock of Falperra, is seated a small tower, and chapel, dedicated to our Lady of the Pillar. This was the position of the French on the night of the 15th instant, and the

Marshal Duke of Dalmatia, was glad to accept the shelter of a miserable hovel, which stood by the road side. The towers of a convent rising out of the wood on the brow of a fine commanding eminence, claimed attention from its beautiful situation. Braga is watered by two small streams, the Cavedo and the Deste.

The country in the vicinity is richly wooded, and the well cultivated fields already give promise of an abundant harvest. This city is the see of an archbishop, who disputes the primacy with Toledo. The cathedral is a handsome structure of the Corinthian, having been rebuilt in that order of architecture about a century before. The original was gothic, of which only one chancel remains. On the first entrance of the French into the north of Portugal, the archbishop directed the sacred symbols of their religion, to be buried under ground.

The expulsion of the French, from the handsome city of Oporto, was the signal for the revival of commerce, and the lively bustle of the now thronged streets, formed an agreeable contrast with its appearance, about a fortnight ago. The cruelty of the French is spoken of with the utmost detestation. On their first arrival, the unarmed inhabitants who happened to be in the streets, were bayoneted without distinction of age or sex. Loison is universally execrated by the Portuguese, as the author of this inhuman massacre.

The foreign merchants residing in this city, are particularly hospitable and attentive to strangers, who would otherwise be much at a loss; as the higher ranks in Portugal are little inclined to associate even with each other. This may, in some degree, be accounted for by the extreme indolence, which forms a prominent feature in the character of this nation, and is repugnant to the laws of polished society.

The Portuguese are more superstitious than the inhabitants of any other Catholic country, and are remarkably fond of all religious processions and ceremonies. Few houses are without a private chapel, in which mass is celebrated at least once a day; hence the incredible number of the clergy. Every family has a confessor, who not only takes care of their spiritual concerns, but the domestic arrangements also are often under his controul.

No people in the world are more docile and submissive to the order of their magistrates and superiors; and this ready obedience was found of the greatest consequence, as facilitating in many instances, the operations of the campaign.

They are remarkably sober, and seldom indulge in any excess. The men wrapped up in long cloaks at all seasons, amuse themselves for hours in looking out of the windows, while the women are actively employed in attending to their household concerns.

In their demeanour towards strangers and each other, they are extremely courteous, and it is no uncommon thing to see peasants conversing with their heads uncovered, in token of natural respect.

The Portuguese have always been considered the most jealous nation in the world, and not without reason; for they keep their wives in the greatest restraint, which treatment is sure to produce aversion and disgust.

In general, the women of this country have a decent, and most respectable carriage, and there is nothing in their exterior appearance to proclaim the least impropriety of conduct; yet it is well known, they make amends for the tyranny of their husbands, by occasionally listening, without scruple, to the vows of a lover.

LETTER XI.

March of the British to the South of Portugal.—Monastery of Grijon, Pinhiero, Albegaria Velha, and Adega.—Halt at Coimbra.

Coimbra, 4th June, 1809.

On the 28th of May, soon after daybreak, the guards marched from Oporto, and before noon, the 3d regiment halted at the monastery of Grijon, in a beautiful and finely wooded situation, about four miles from the sea, to which there is a gentle descent. The monks were regular canons of the rich order of St. Augustine. At their desire, the provisions were given to the cooks of the convent, and about 4 o'clock, the officers sat down to dinner in the Refectory. The repast was but indifferent, nothing being added by the good fathers, who, in excuse, pleaded poverty, and alledged the French had stript them of every thing.—Next day, the brigade halted at Pinhieros, 4 leagues—30th, at Albegaria Velha, 3 leagues—31st, reached Adega, a small town on the banks of a beautiful stream. The Coldstream was

quartered in the adjacent village of Sardao.—
On the following day, halted. June the
2d, the guards marched to Malheada, 2
leagues and a half distant from Coimbra,
where they arrived about 10 o'clock yesterday. The men occupy convents, the officers
are quartered upon the inhabitants, who
received them with kindness and hospitality.

The amiable sisterhood of St. Clare, partook in the general satisfaction, at the intelligence of Sir Arthur Wellesley's successful
operations against the enemy in the north
of Portugal, as they had felt considerable
alarm on the first arrival of the French, for
the safety of their peaceful and splendid
establishment.

In a day or two, the British continue their
march to the South, Abrantes having been
fixed upon as the head quarters of the army.

LETTER XII.

Through Condiexa and Pombal to Leyria, Ourem.—City of Thomar.—Arrive at Punhete.—Reflections on the Campaign.

Punhete on the Tagus, 18*th June,* 1809.

ON the morning of the 6th instant, the guards and General Cameron's brigade, marched from Coimbra, and passing through Condiexa and Pombal as on the former route, the guards reached Leyria on the 3d day. Brigadier-General Cameron marched by a road to the left of these towns.

On the 9th to Ourem, 4 leagues of a very indifferent cross road. The column was detained considerably by the brigade of artillery: ten horses with difficulty dragged each of the guns up the steep bank of the Leyes. The little town of Ourem is beautifully situated on the side of a hill, whose summit was crowned by the ruins of an ancient Moorish castle.

June the 10th, to Thomar, 3 leagues; the road as yesterday. This city was for some time, the head quarters of the Portuguese army, under Marshal Beresford. The brigade was quartered in a fine old convent, which is supplied with water by a superb aquaduct, constructed for the purpose by Philip the 3d. The church, which is approached by a noble flight of steps, is a pure and costly remain of the Arabesque. It contains some beautiful paintings; particularly a Magdalen in one of the pannels: the wood work of the choir, is carved in a rich and inimitable style.

On the 11th, the guards arrived in the small town of Punhete, beautifully situated at the confluence of the Zezere with the Tagus.—A bridge of boats lay across the former river.

The whole of the army has been assembled in this neighbourhood; Major-General Mackenzie's division forms the advance, and Colonel Donkin's brigade has proceeded to Castel-Branco. Reinforcements are daily expected from England, and it is the general opinion, that the commander of the forces intends to advance into Spain; Victor having retired from the frontier towards Madrid. Mean time, the most active preparations are making to re-equip the army for the field.

A few reflections naturally occur on the present situation of affairs. Six weeks have scarcely elapsed since Sir Arthur Wellesley assumed the command of the army. At this period, Marshal Soult, with a force of 24,000 men, was in possession of Oporto and the whole of the north of Portugal; while Victor, with a superior army, hung upon the eastern frontier, and might be expected to interpose betwixt the rear of the British and Lisbon, the moment of their advance beyond the Mondego. Notwithstanding this imposing attitude of Victor's army, the commander of the forces promptly decided on attacking the force under Marshal Soult. Leaving a corps of observation to watch the motions of the former, he directed his principal attention to the north; which, in the course of a few days, was completely freed from the presence and dominion of the enemy. After allowing his troops a short repose, Sir Arthur Wellesley hastened to place his army on the line of the Tagus; and this operation was effected with a rapidity which has seldom been equalled, even in the annals of modern warfare. Marshal Victor, on receiving intelligence of

Soult's discomfiture and subsequent retreat into Gallicia, commenced his march for the neighbourhood of Madrid, so that, out of the 50,000 French who lately threatened and infested Portugal, not a man is left. It is but too much the fashion, to estimate the importance of any enterprize by the loss which is incurred in atchieving it; but this is frequently an unjust criterion, certainly not a fair one, in regard to the services of this army, which have been of the most useful and brilliant description, as the result has indubitably proved.

The several brigades of infantry are now formed into 4 divisions, under the command of the senior general officers with each.

1st division, Lieutenant-General Sherbrooke, is composed of—

    The brigade of guards,
    Brigadier-General Cameron's brigade,
    King's German Legion.

2d division—

    Major-General Hill,
    Brigadier-General R. Stewart.

3d division—

    Major-General Mackenzie,
    Colonel Donkin.

4th division—

    Brigadier-General A. Campbell,
    Colonel Peacoche.

Colonel Peacoche being appointed commander of Lisbon, was succeeded in the command of his brigade by Colonel Kemmis.

LETTER XIII.

Advance of the British into Spain.—The Guards reach to Castel Branco, through Abrantes, Corticado, Sobriera Formosa, and Sazedas.

Castel Branco, 2d July, 1809.

THE situation of the enemy having been perfectly ascertained by intelligence from General Cuesta, Sir Arthur Wellesley advanced with the army from Abrantes on the 28th of June, in several divisions, and by different routes; the country through which the line of march lay, being unfavourable to the movements of large bodies, from the difficulty of procuring supplies.

The 2d division, under the orders of Major-General Hill, and the German legion on successive days with the artillery, marched along the south bank of the Tagus, which they crossed at Villa Velha, by a bridge of boats. Brigadier-General A. Campbell's route was on the north side, and the march of the guards and General Cameron's brigade, forming part of Lieutenant-General

Sherbrooke's division, was on the direct road to the frontier by which Junot entered the kingdom, and experienced such difficulties as obliged him to destroy a great number of his guns.

After a pleasant halt of a fortnight, the guards marched from Punhete on the 27th of June, and reached Abrantes, two leagues distant, by 9 o'clock.—Latter part of the road extremely hilly —The 3d regiment was quartered in the convent of *Religieuses of St. Clare*.

At half-past 1 on the following morning the generale beat, and by 3 the column was formed on the road leading to Castel Branco. At 9 the troops halted and hutted in a wood of pines near the village of St. Domingo.

June the 29th the troops advanced at the same early hour as on the preceding day; and about 4 halted in the little town of Costiçada. This day's march was six leagues, the road very hilly, and the troops in consequence were much fatigued. About 2 o'clock a tremendous thunder storm came on, accompanied with lightning and heavy rain. The Coldstream and General Cameron's brigade halted at Cardagos, seven miles in the rear.

June the 30th, at half-past 4 A. M. the 3d regiment marched, and about 8 o'clock reached the miserable village of Sobriera Formosa, 2 leagues; where being joined by the Coldstream, at 11 the column advanced to Sazedas, 4 leagues beyond. At 1 the troops defiled through the strong pass of Montegordo, defended by several redoubts, and a Portuguese battalion; and soon after crossed the river Alvito, knee-deep. At 5 P. M. halted and went into very indifferent quarters. The town was completely deserted by the inhabitants, who had fled to the mountains with all their effects, by order of the government, on the French making their appearance at Alcantara. Next day the brigade moved out of the town to the side of an adjoining hill, and constructed huts. At 2 this morning the guards were again on march, and arrived at Castel Branco, 3 leagues, about 11 o'clock. The troops were hutted a mile beyond the city. The country around Castel Branco is fertile, and abounds in cattle.

In general the roads of Portugal are in very bad order, and the distances between towns computed in an arbitrary manner, as the league varies in length from 3 to 7 miles.—The patriotic cares of the Marquis de Pombal for the improvement of his native country, had suggested the necessity of good roads throughout the kingdom; but since that minister's decease none of his many excellent plans have been adopted.

The reports current here are, that the French have concentrated their forces at Talavera, to the amount of 45,000 men, of which number Joseph Buonaparte had brought 6,000 from Madrid, after pillaging the city.

LETTER XIV.

The British enter Spain at Zarza Major, and arrive at Placentia, where the whole of the army is concentrated.

Placentia, 16th July, 1809.

At half-past 1 on the morning of the 3d instant, Lieutenant-General Sherbrooke's division was in motion on the road to the frontier, and about noon halted at Lodiero, a village consisting of a few houses, 4 leagues distant from Castel Branco—the road very good.—On the march the column forded the Ponsul, where Junot lost 200 men, it being much swoln at the time of his advance into Portugal.

July the 4th. To Zibriera 3 short leagues. The troops contrived to *bivouac* at the end of each day's march, and were particularly fortunate in having fine weather throughout.

July the 5th, at half-past 2 A.M. the column was in motion, and after a march of 2 leagues passed the frontier town of Salvatierra, situated on an eminence. Soon after, fording the small river Elja, which here forms the boundary of the two kingdoms, the division entered the Spanish territory, and proceeding over an uncultivated plain, arrived at Zarza Major, 3 miles from the river, about 10 o'clock. The troops went into the huts which had been constructed by Major-General Mackenzie's division, a league beyond the town: here they halted until the morning of the 7th, when the division moved forward about 2 o'clock. This day's march was through a delightful country, part of an ancient royal forest. At 10 halted and hutted within a mile of the town of Montalegar, situated on the banks of the Allagon, over which there is a good bridge of 7 arches. This little place had an appearance of cleanliness superior to what was usually seen in the villages of Portugal; it had once been fortified, but the works were now in a ruinous state.

July the 8th. At 1 this morning the column advanced, and about 8 o'clock passed through Coria, a town of some note, and hutted for the night in a wood, about a mile beyond. A column of dust on the road to Placentia, marked the route of

General Hill's division.—Coria stands in an elevated situation, and about a quarter of a mile distant runs the Allagon, which an earthquake had caused to desert its former channel, so that a handsome bridge of 5 arches is now rendered useless. At the entrance of the town is a monastery of Franciscans, whose personal appearance certainly bespoke the poverty of their order.

July the 9th. An hour after midnight the generale beat, and the column, left in front, passed under an arch of the bridge, and proceeded on the road to Placentia. At noon the troops forded the Allagon, which was attended with some delay, as the river runs broad and deep. About 1 halted and hutted on the side of a hill facing the town of Galisteo, at the distance of a mile on the south bank of the Xerte. The division remained on this ground the two following days. On the 10th a report reached the camp of the Spanish army, commanded by General Blake, having been defeated by Suchet. Sir Arthur Wellesley had gone from Placentia, accompanied by Colonel Murray, Quarter-Master General, to hold a conference with Cuesta, whose head-quarters are at Almaraz, on the Tagus; his advance under the Duke of Albuquerque at Arzobispo.

On the 12th of July the division marched to Placentia, 10 miles of good road. The peasantry in this district were employed in cutting down the corn.

The division after crossing the bridge over the Xerte, passed under the walls of the city to a wood about a league distant, and hutted. The whole of the infantry, except Major-General Mackenzie's division, which continued to form the advance, was assembled on this ground.

The city of Placentia has many remains of Moorish architecture, particularly the great church; it is completely walled round with circular towers at short distances, but unprovided with cannon, and the works are mouldering rapidly into decay. The streets are narrow, yet the houses are of a good stile, and have a pleasing air of cleanliness.

There are two bridges over the Xerte, one of seven handsome arches. Water is conveyed into the city by an aqueduct of very ancient construction.

A striking difference is already perceived betwixt the personal appearance and manners of the Portuguese and Spaniards, clearly in favour of the latter, who seem of a more manly character.

Provisions are tolerably plentiful, and vegetables in abundance. Indeed the district of Placentia is considered one of the most luxuriant in Spain. Wine is brought into the camp daily in great quantities, but of an inferior quality.—By a wise regulation the price of every article is settled by the Alcades, and affixed in the market place to prevent imposition.

Ice is procured from the mountains, at the foot of which the troops were encamped. Even at this advanced season their tops are covered with snow.

In a valley not far from the city, stands the celebrated Jeromite convent of St. Juste, into which Charles V. after alarming all Europe for upwards of a century, by the terror of his arms, retired with a few domestics to end his days in penitence and prayer.

This day the 1st battalion of the 48th regiment, commanded by Lieutenant-Colonel Donelan, marched into camp in 18 days from Lisbon, leaving only four men sick on the road.

LETTER XV.

The British form a Juncture with Cuesta's Army, and arrive at Talavera de la Reyna.—Position of the French, and Plan of the intended Attack.

Talavera de la Reyna, 22d July, 1809.

An hour before day-light, on the 17th of July, the British quitted Placentia, and after a march of two leagues, the infantry halted near Malpartida de Placentia, on a plain, where was not a single bush to shelter the troops from the scorching heat of the sun. Water was very scarce and bad.

Brigadier General Fane, with the brigade of heavy cavalry, was advanced 2 leagues in front.

July the 18th, the army moved from their ground at half-past 3 in the morning, and in four hours reached the Tietar, which was crossed by a temporary bridge; the one of boats being rendered unserviceable by the Spanish peasantry, on the appearance of the French. At 2 P. M. the troops halted, and hutted close to the river. The commander of the forces, with his staff, passed the column to Mayadas, a small village about a mile beyond. General Cuesta's army crossed the Tagus this morning at Almaraz, according to the place of operations concerted betwixt him and Sir Arthur Wellesley. And Sir Robert Wilson, whose corps had hitherto preceded the advance of the British, moved by a road to the left, after passing the Tietar.

A little wine was this day brought into camp by the peasantry, but nothing besides.

July the 19th, the army was again in motion before day-light, and proceeded until noon along the banks of the Tietar, in a line parallel with the march of the Spanish army. The heat of the sun had been extremely oppressive for these three days past. After a march of twelve hours, the troops halted in a beautiful wood, near the village of Centinello. It was generally understood, that the French out-posts were at the distance of only 3 leagues from the advance of the British under Major General Mackenzie, who, supported by General Fane's brigade of heavy cavalry, was about three miles in front of the main body.

By the latest information received of the enemy, it appeared that Victor had made the following disposition of his forces, amounting, according to report, to about 30,000 men.

His advanced guard of cavalry occupied the city of Talavera de la Reyna.

His right flanked by a rising ground, and secured by heavy artillery, rested upon the Alberche, which protected his front, the line being extended along the banks of that river to the Tagus, and eastward in the direction of Toledo; in the neighbourhood of which city, Venegas, who had been detached by Cuesta, with 18,000 men, was directed to arrive on the 24th instant.

The intended plan of attack was formed on this information.

General Cuesta's army supported by the British cavalry, was to force the bridge over the Alberche, and attack the left of the enemy whilst the British infantry forded the river in front, and endeavoured to turn his right.

Venegas, after gaining possession of Toledo, in which the enemy was supposed to have left a very inconsiderable force, was to pass the Tagus, and place himself betwixt Madrid and the rear of the French army, co-operating if possible, with Sir Robert Wilson, who had been for some days at Escalona, with the Lusitanian legion, consisting of 2000 infantry, 500 cavalry, and a few field pieces. Sir Robert had succeeded in opening a communication with the capital.

July the 20th, the army moved forward at 3 in the morning; and on leaving the wood, entered a long extensive plain, which reached to Oropesa, 6 leagues distant. About 4 o'clock the column halted a mile beyond the town, after a most fatiguing march. A strong piquet of French cavalry had been here on the preceding evening; and at their departure this morning, they plundered the town, and carried off all the bread and wine they could find.

In the course of this afternoon, Cuesta's advanced guard entered Oropesa, and the junction of the two armies was effected.

July the 21st, the generale beat at the usual early hour, but after the troops were under arms, the march was suspended to give time for the Spanish army to take a position in front of the British. About half-past 10 o'clock the army of Estremadura halted to refresh, at the distance of half a league, in number 35,000, including 7000 cavalry. The infantry appeared strong able bodied men, but deficient in discipline. They are the same troops who behaved so well at the battle of Medellin, on which occasion the conduct of the infantry was cool and resolute, and they positively turned the left wing of Victor's army; but the cavalry gave way when their services were most wanted.

At 4 in the afternoon the whole of the troops were drawn out, and General Cuesta, with his adjutant-general O'Donaghue, accompanied by Sir Arthur Wellesley and his staff, reviewed the British line.

The Spanish leader appeared an infirm old man, so much so that he is obliged to be lifted into his saddle; and as he cannot remain long at a time on horseback, an ancient family coach drawn by 6 mules, is in constant attendance.

General Cuesta is said to possess the entire confidence of his troops, and this may

be the reason why he has been selected to
command an army of patriots, which ought
to have an officer of youth, vigour, and
talent at its head. The Duke of Albuquerque
who commands the cavalry, is esteemed an
active officer, zealous in the cause of his
country. Report speaks highly of the military talents of General O'Donaghue.

This morning the combined army was in
motion before day-break, and advanced
along the extensive plain towards Talavera.
Few officers had ever previously seen so large
a body acting as if by one impulse, and
marching in one direction. It was in truth a
sublime and magnificent spectacle, and the
occasion was calculated to excite the most
exalted ideas in a soldier's bosom.

About 6 o'clock a heavy cannonade commenced in front, and continued at intervals
until 3 in the afternoon; a little before which
the combined army *bivouaced* within a mile
and a half of Talavera, whence the enemy
was dislodged in the course of the morning,
by the advance of the British and Spaniards.
The French cavalry retreated over the Alberche closely pursued.

LETTER XVI.

The Combined Army moves from the Wood of Olives, to the Banks of the Alberche.—Retreat of Marshal Victor.—British Out-posts at Caselegas.—The Spaniards occupy Santa Olalla.

Talavera de la Reyna, 26th July, 1809.

EXACTLY at 4 in the morning of the 23d instant, the several divisions of the army moved out of the wood in which they had reposed the preceding night, and were halted almost immediately afterwards. At 8 o'clock the troops again advanced, and about noon, arrived near the ruins of an old convent, within 2 miles of the Alberche, on the opposite bank of which the enemy was posted in force, when an order was given for the British to return to their former ground. This unexpected movement occasioned a variety of reports and surmises. By some it was said, that Sir Arthur Wellesley and Cuesta had disagreed, and the Spaniards were averse to engage on a Sunday; others asserted that the preparations of the latter, were not complete, and that he waited for ammunition : however, it was generally understood, that the position of the French was to be attacked on the following morning.

An hour after midnight, on the 24th of July, the army assembled without beat of drum, and advanced left in front, in silence and with the most perfect regularity to the expected attack. About 6 the guards arrived within sight of the Alberche, when they perceived with surprise, that the enemy had abandoned his position, and was in full retreat. The commander of the forces, and Lieutenant General Sherbrooke had passed the Alberche with a considerable body of cavalry, and Major General Mackenzie's division of infantry, and hung on the rear of the enemy's retiring columns. The advance of the British halted at the village of Caselegas, 1 league beyond the Alberche. Cuesta pushed forward his out-posts, 2 leagues further to Santa Olalla, late the head-quarters of Marshal Victor.

After halting for orders until noon, during which interval, the officers crossed the rear to see the French huts, which were remarkable for their neatness and regularity; the troops returned to their former position, on the Wood of Olives. It was now a subject of general regret that the French had not been attacked on the preceding day, even without the co-operation of the Spaniards. Whatever was the real cause of this retrograde movement, the disappointment of the troops at not being led against the enemy, whom they had made so many harassing marches to come up with, was very apparent. An advance however, at the present moment, was doubtless rendered either unnecessary or impracticable from circumstances, which were known only to the commander of the forces. Indeed the difficulty of procuring supplies for so large an army might have proved an insuperable obstacle. So far hitherto, had success attended the movements of the allies, that the enemy found himself compelled to quit his position on the Alberche, which the appearance of Cuesta's force alone would never have effected.

In the course of this day, the conduct of the Spanish leader was very generally commented upon. He was considered a man of strict honour, and to possess an invincible hatred to the French; but his dilatory and half digested measures did not seem calculated to be of much service to his country.

Talavera de la Reyna is a large town with several handsome streets, but an air of desolation and ruin reigned throughout; many of the houses were deserted, and the appearance of the whole place presented a sad picture of the ravages of war, which seemed to have been in a peculiar manner inflicted on this devoted town. The French troops during their stay, had been guilty of the greatest excesses; a number of houses were completely destroyed, and the furniture burnt for fuel. In every quarter were to be seen marks of the devastation they had committed, which must have imprinted a lasting hatred in the minds of the unfortunate inhabitants. Even the satisfaction felt by those who remained in the town at being delivered from an enemy who had caused them so much misery and vexation, could not prevent an air of melancholy from appearing in their countenances on viewing the destruction of property and the havoc made on all sides. The Plaza de Toros, where the bull-fights and other exhibitions were held, was now a scene of the greatest desolation. In contemplating the spot where the Spaniards enjoyed their national amusements, it was impossible not to feel regret at the sad change that had taken place.

The cathedral, a handsome modern building, remained uninjured; the French being contented with carrying off the splendid ornaments used in their ceremonies of religion. A very fine altar-piece by Murillo, excited universal admiration. In the church of St. Antonio, the enemy destroyed every thing, and converted it into a barrack for infantry.

LETTER XVII.

Battle of Talavera.—Positions of the Respective Armies.—The Enemy foiled in his repeated Attempts to turn the left of the British makes a Grand Attack upon the right and centre.— General Sherbrooke's Division advances to the charge with bayonets.—The Brigade of Guards having advanced too far under a heavy fire, sustain a considerable loss, and retire, covered by the first battalion of the 48th Regiment. The French retreat during the night.—On the following morning General Robert Crawford's Brigade of Light Infantry arrived.

Talavera de la Reyna, 29th July, 1809.

ON the 26th instant, a heavy cannonade commenced soon after day-light, and continued until 4 in the afternoon, when the commander of the forces, who had rode out at an early hour, returned from the field in high spirits. The action was betwixt the advance of the French and the Spanish out-posts, which fell back upon the position heretofore occupied by the enemy on the **Alberche**. The Spaniards lost from 3 to 400 in killed and wounded; several of the latter were brought into Talavera in the course of the afternoon.

The cannonade was renewed next morning, the 27th; and the Spaniards, covered by the British cavalry and Major-General Mackenzie's division of infantry, continued to retire upon the town. As the day advanced, the intention of the enemy to try the issue of a general engagement became no longer doubtful; and about 3 P. M. his columns, which moved forward after crossing the Alberche with great rapidity, having approached within 2 leagues of Talavera, the several divisions of the British army were placed in the positions previously chosen, where they remained awaiting the attack.

Brigadier-General Alexander Campbell, with two brigades of infantry, was posted on the right, near an unfinished redoubt; the Guards, General Cameron's brigade, and the King's German Legion, formed the centre, under Lieutenant-General Sherbrooke, and Major-General Hill's division extended along the rising grounds on the left, flanked by a heavy battery. Major-General Mackenzie, who commanded the advance, had previously withdrawn his troops after the whole of the Spaniards re-crossed the Alberche; and this movement was executed with the utmost judgment and ability by that gallant officer. His division formed a second line in rear of the centre.

The cavalry was commanded by Lieutenant-General Payne. Major-General Cotton's light brigade, supported the right and centre, Brigadier-General Anson's and the heavy brigade under General Fane, were on the left.

Brigadier-General Howarth commanded the royal artillery, and the several batteries were under the superintendance of Lieutenant-Colonels Robe and Framlingham.

The ground in front of the British was principally open, but intersected with roads leading to the town, and the bed of a small river, which had been formed by the winter torrents, and was at present dry.

The Spanish infantry formed in two lines, and supported by the king's regiment of cavalry, were posted behind the mud enclosures of the olive grounds and vineyards, extending from the right of General Alexander Campbell's position, to the suburbs and town of Talavera, which they also occupied, having their right flanked by the Tagus.

The Duke of Albuquerque was in rear of the left of the whole line, with the main body of the Spanish cavalry, and Lieutenant-General Don Luis Bassecourt was subsequently placed with about 3,000 light troops in the valley below the left of the British, to keep in check, a body of the enemy who appeared in the mountains beyond, which were, however, at too great a distance to have any effect upon the impending contest.

The Spanish army was commanded by Cuesta, General in chief, and the several divisions of infantry were under the orders of Lieutenant-Generals Don Francisco de Eguia, second in command, the Marquis del Partago, Don Rafael Maglano, and Don Juan de Henestrosa.

The French army, in number nearly 50,000 strong, was commanded by Marshal Victor, assisted by Marshal Jourdain and General Sebastiani, under the direction of Joseph Buonaparte, in person.

About half-past 6 o'clock, the enemy appeared in considerable force on the heights opposite the centre of the British line, and opened a heavy cannonade of shot and shells, which was instantaneously returned from the principal battery placed on a commanding eminence in the rear of General Hill's division. At the same time, the French made a vigorous attack on the left, where after a most obstinate conflict, they were completely repulsed at the point of the bayonet. The enemy also pushed forward several corps of infantry, supported by a strong division of cavalry on the right, with a view of carrying the town of Talavera, in which object he failed, and was driven back by the fire from the Spanish batteries. The cannonade continued on both sides until dusk.

In the course of the night the enemy made a second assault upon the height; from whence, after gaining a momentary possession he was dislodged by General Hill, with prodigious slaughter.

At 2 in the morning the Spanish line was alarmed at all points, by the approach of the enemy's light troops, who were received with a brisk discharge of musquetry, which ceased in about 10 minutes, when the silence of night again prevailed on the field of battle.

At length day-light broke upon the contending armies, who were drawn up opposite to each other in the positions they respectively occupied at the beginning of the action on the preceding evening. About 6 the engagement was renewed, and continued without intermission, until 11 o'clock, when the firing ceased, as if by mutual consent, for nearly three hours, during which interval, the French appeared to be employed in cooking, and the British army reposed on the ground, seemingly regardless of the enemy's presence. It was at this time also the wounded were carried off to the rear, and while engaged in this painful duty, the British and French soldiers shook hands with each other, and expressed their admiration of the gallantry displayed by the troops of both nations. The principal efforts of the French throughout the morning were again directed upon the left; but Major-General Hill successfully repelled every attempt to turn his position, and obliged the enemy to retire with considerable loss.

Sir Arthur Wellesley with his staff, observed the progress of the battle on a height to the left of the British line. From this point he witnessed every movement that was made, and in the midst of the hottest fire issued the necessary orders with his characteristic coolness and judgment. Two of his Aides-de-Camp, Captains Bouverie and Burgh, were wounded by his side.

At 1 P. M. the enemy was observed bringing up fresh troops and forming his columns, apparently for the purpose of renewing the action; and in fact about 2 o'clock, the French again advanced under a heavy cannonade, and made a general attack upon the whole of the position occupied by the British.

The enemy's attacking columns on the right had arrived within a short distance of the unfinished redoubt, when General Alexander Campbell made a vigorous charge with his division, supported by two battalions of Spanish infantry, and drove them back with the loss of their artillery.

The efforts of the enemy on the left were equally unsuccessful as before, and a charge made by Brigadier-General Anson with the 23d light dragoons and German hussars, upon a solid column of infantry, although attended with a severe loss to the former regiment, had the effect of checking their further advance in that direction.

Meanwhile the centre was warmly engaged. Exactly at 3 o'clock several heavy columns advanced upon this point, and deployed with the utmost precision into line as they entered the plain, which lay betwixt the heights occupied by the hostile armies. This was the grand attack, and on the first indication of the enemy's intention, General Sherbrooke gave directions that his division should prepare for the charge. At this awful moment all was silent, except a few guns of the enemy, answered by the British artillery on the hill. The French came on over the rough and broken ground in the valley, in the most imposing manner and with great resolution, and were met by the British with their usual undaunted firmness. As if with one accord the division advanced against the enemy, whose ranks were speedily broken, and thrown into confusion by a well directed volley. The impetuosity of the soldiers was not to be repressed; and the brigade on the immediate left of the guards being halted, that flank from its advanced situation in the eagerness of pursuit, became exposed to the enemy,. who had already given way, and deserted his guns on the hill in front, until observing this part of the line unsupported, the French rallied, and returned with increased numbers to their attack upon the centre.

Brigadier-General Harry Campbell now gave orders for the guards to retire to their original position in line, and the 1st battalion of the 48th regiment was directed to cover this movement by the Commander of the Forces, who saw and provided for every emergency during the tremendous conflict. Foiled at all points, the French withdrew the remains of the columns which had been unsuccessfully opposed to the centre; they however continued the fire of their artillery, and the engagement which had been renewed this morning with the rising of the sun, ceased only with its setting.

About 6 in the evening, the long dry grass having caught fire, the flames spread rapidly over the field of action, and consumed in their fatal progress numbers of the dead and wounded.

A dim and cheerless moon threw a feint lustre over the surrounding objects after the close of day. Small parties were sent out to bring in the wounded; the enemy was employed in a similar manner, and had made large fires along the whole front of his extensive line.

The troops lay upon their arms this second night, without provisions of any kind—water even was scarce. It was fully expected that the French would renew the attack in the morning, but they retired under cover of the night, leaving in the hands of the British 20 pieces of artillery, and some prisoners. Their rear guard, consisting of cavalry, alone remained on the right bank of the Alberche at day-break. The retreat was certainly conducted with ability, and was not generally known in the British army until long after the enemy had abandoned his position.

This brilliant victory, over an enemy so infinitely superior in numbers, has not been achieved without a considerable loss both of valuable officers and men. That of the enemy, however, to judge from the appearance of the field, must be immense.

Soon after 8 o'clock, the British quitted their positions in the field, and again hutted in the Wood of Olives. About 9 the light brigade under General Robert Crawford arrived, having marched 12 Spanish leagues in the preceding 24 hours.

LETTER XVIII.

Information received from a French Officer taken prisoner.— Report of Marshal Soult advancing on Placentia.

Talavera de la Reyna, 1st August, 1809.

MOTIVES of curiosity induced several officers to visit Talavera on the afternoon of the 29th of July. The town appeared almost deserted; here and there a few soldiers were walking about, looking for the quarters of their wounded comrades. The houses were for the greater part shut up; the inhabitants previous to the engagement, had fled across the Tagus with their most valuable effects, and were not yet returned.

The French are said to be continuing their retreat. From an officer who was taken prisoner on the banks of the Tagus, the following information has been obtained:

When the combined army arrived in front of Talavera on the 22d of July,

Marshal Victor's force amounted to	28,000
Joined him from Toledo . .	8,000
Carried forward	6,000

Brought forward	36,000
On the 25th two regiments of cavalry, the 14th and 26th infantry	3,000
Joseph Buonaparte arrived on the afternoon of the 27th, with the guards from Madrid	8,000
Total number of the enemy engaged	47,000

Joseph retreated on the evening of the 28th, and slept at Caselegas.

On the 29th his guards moved forward to Santa Olalla, when they halted for the night	8,000
Late on that day a division was sent off towards Toledo of	9,000
Killed and wounded on the 27th and 28th, fully	*8,000
Remains with Victor	22,000

The above facts stated by this officer accord with the information received from two dragoons taken with him, examined separately, and also with the intelligence obtained from the Alcalde at Cebolla, who is known by the

---

* It is certain the loss of the French in killed and wounded was at least 14,000.

magistrates to be a true patriot; to a certainty Joseph is off, but whether to Madrid or Toledo this officer does not know. It is equally certain that a strong division was sent off on the evening of the 29th, to sustain Toledo.

Sebastiani had a command in the battle, and Marshal Jourdain remained with Joseph Buonaparte until he quitted the field. Victor commanded under the immediate direction of Joseph.

The French army is in the greatest distress for provisions, and the troops have had little bread from the day they were first driven out of Talavera, and none from the 27th until the 31st, when four thousand pounds of biscuit arrived from Madrid, and a farther supply was expected, but is supposed to have been taken. The whole of the French from Victor down to the lowest soldier, are discontented with the war in Spain, and all wish to return to their own country.

On the arrival of Joseph on the 27th, he publicly reproached Victor for not having beaten or taken the British and Spanish armies already, and assured the army that this should be done on the 28th. He was seen on the evening of that day retiring from the field, the picture of melancholy and disappointment.

This prisoner heard Victor say, on the afternoon of the 28th, that he felt himself abandoned by Soult. On the 30th it was known in the French army that the latter was coming round by Placentia with 12,000 men.

When the troops came from Toledo to join Victor, there were only 1500 left in that city, and Joseph withdrew the whole of the garrison from Madrid, except about 3000 men, of whom a part were stationed in the fort of El Retiro.

It caused much consternation in the French army to hear, during the engagement, that Toledo was bombarded by Venegas, (whose operations were restrained by an order of the Junta,) and that the British had been reinforced by General Crawford's division.

General Morlot was killed, and Lapice received a mortal wound on the 28th, of which he died the next day. An immense number of Colonels and Field Officers were killed and wounded; and the oldest soldiers in the French army declared the day after the action that they had never seen more determined fighting; and all agreed that in the war with Spain this was the first time they had met with soldiers. They wondered where the Spaniards were; as their position was covered with wood, our allies were not seen by the French.

The sick and wounded of the army are in a shocking state; and this prisoner thinks the retreat is suspended to give as much time as possible to send away the wounded, which is almost impracticable, as they have scarcely any means of conveyance.

All letters from France are opened by order of Joseph Buonaparte, and those burned which contain bad news. The French army, however, has heard of Napoleon's defeat in Austria.

The report of this day is, that Marshal Soult is advancing with 12 or 15,000 men on Placentia, from which he was only 10 leagues distant on the 30th ultimo.

LETTER XIX.

Retreat of the Combined Army, to the South Bank of the Tagus.—Particulars of the March.—Cuesta resigns his Command.—The British Prisoners of War treated with great humanity by Marshal Mortier.

Banks of the Elmonte, 14th August, 1809.

It is now necessary to turn from a consideration of the splendid victory obtained over the troops of France, on the plains of Talavera, to a relation of the events which caused a gallant and successful British army to retire precipitately, from the scene of their late triumphs, and act upon the defensive.

During the stay of the army at Talavera, both before and after the action, the supplies of every kind had been very insufficient, and the inhabitants of that town evinced no disposition to relieve the wants of the British, and to accommodate the sick and wounded. Their removal from Talavera therefore, was become an object of too much interest to be any longer delayed, particularly, as by Marshal Soult's arrival at Placentia.

the provisions expected from that quarter, and for which arrangements were made by the commissariat, had fallen into the enemy's hands.

On the morning of the 3d of August, the British army moved from Talavera; but for an hour after the troops were under arms, they remained uncertain, whether it was Sir Arthur Wellesley's intention to advance upon Madrid, or proceed against Marshal Soult, in the contrary direction. Their doubts, however, were soon at an end, for on leaving the Wood of Olives, the army began to retrace its former steps, and about 2 in the afternoon again halted near the town of Oropesa. Although by this retrogade movement, the British were of necessity compelled to leave behind a considerable number of their sick and wounded, yet less anxiety was felt on this account, as they relied on the Spaniards keeping Victor in check, should he, on being informed of Sir Arthur Wellesley's departure, again attempt to advance : besides, under any circumstances, it would not have been consistent with humanity, to have attempted the removal of more of the sick and wounded than were really brought off.

Cuesta, whose force remained nearly entire, having taken little share in the action, promised to maintain the position which the British had so successfully defended, but in a few hours after their march, the Spanish leader abandoned his post, and, with the whole of his army, followed the route of the British.

This conduct of General Cuesta, increased the embarrasments of the situation in which the British army was already placed by Marshal Soult's arrival at Placentia, and all hopes of any effectual co-operation being now at an end, the commander of the forces determined to withdraw his troops over the bridge of Arzobispo, with a view of covering Saville and the South of Spain, and at the same time, to preserve the communication open with Lisbon.

In pursuance of these objects, on the following morning the march was resumed, and after having experienced considerable difficulties and privations, the whole of the British army arrived in the valley watered by the Elmonte, on the 11th instant.

Although there can be no pleasure in dwelling on the particulars of a march performed under such circumstances, yet, perhaps, a detail of the daily progress made by the British troops, through these inhospitable mountains, may prove somewhat interesting.

At day-break on the 4th instant, the troops were under arms, but did not move from the ground on which they *bivouaced* until 9 o'clock. A very small quantity of bread was issued to the army, which then marched down 2 leagues to the bridge of Arzobispo, and crossing the Tagus, halted for the night, on the opposite bank. It was reported, that the Spaniards on the approach of the enemy, had removed the bridge of Almaraz, and many expected the one at this place would have been destroyed, the more effectually to secure the rear.

August the 5th. The troops advanced 6 leagues over a difficult country, and about 4 in the afternoon *bivouaced* on a hill near the village of Valdela Cosa.

August the 6th. This day's march 3 leagues only was through a mountainous district. About noon, the column halted in a romantic spot, near the small river D'Ibor. Several working parties were employed in dragging the artillery up the heights until a late hour.

August the 7th. The country, this day, was even more mountainous and rugged than that through which the army passed yesterday, consequently little progress was made. The heat was excessive, and the troops began to sink under their fatigues. The army had been without bread on the 5th and 6th. A small quantity of flour was received yesterday, but no wine could be procured to raise the drooping spirits and recruit the exhausted strength of the soldiers. Among other reports of the day, it was said, that an officer had crossed the Tagus, and observed the march of the French over the plain, in the direction of Arzobispo.

August the 8th. Although the troops assembled at 4 in the morning, yet the march was deferred nearly 5 hours, to give the artillery time to ascend the heights —About noon, halted on the banks of a small stream, a league from Deleytosa. The villages through which the British had passed, since leaving Arzobispo, were nearly deserted and ruinous.—Not one article of the necessaries of life could be procured in any of them.

August the 9th. At 5 the troops were in motion—About 8 o'clock passed the town of Deleytosa, and halted 2 miles beyond, in a wood on the left of the town of Truxillo, situated on a hill, apparently at the distance of 6 leagues.

A very inadequate proportion of flour and biscuit was issued yesterday, but the troops received a tolerable supply of the latter this morning.

Marshal Soult, after making an unsuccessful attempt to force the bridge of Arzobispo, passed the Tagus with a body of cavalry, at a ford about 2 miles above, and surprised the Spaniards in their position. The latter retreated, after a slight resistance, pursued by the French. It was feared, the whole of their artillery would fall into the enemy's hands. The Duke of Albuquerque, had arrived at head quarters.

In the general orders of this day, the army was informed, that the charge of three-pence per diem only would be made to those troops who had not received their rations regularly, since the 22d of July. During the march, a number of bullocks, sheep and goats were driven forward for the daily consumption of the army. The provisions were cooked overnight for the following day, and being divided into messes, each man carried his dinner in his tin. This was in general the arrangement throughout the campaign.

August the 10th. This day the troops halted, but were kept in readiness to move at a moment's notice. It was asserted, that the French were marching to the South, by the way of Guadaloupe.

August the 11th. Yesterday's halt proved extremely serviceable, from the repose it afforded to the troops and to the horses of the artillery, whose labours had been very severe for some days past —The Spaniards indeed declared, that the road by which the army marched over the mountains, was impracticable, but, contrary to their opinion, the whole of the artillery and stores were ultimately brought forward. Many horses died from fatigue, and the troops, in several places, were obliged to drag the guns and ammunition waggons up the heights.

The troops moved off their ground at daylight, and about eight o'clock, came upon the high road from Madrid to Cadiz, one of the best in Europe; shortly afterwards passed the ruined village of Iaracejo, where are the remains of a Moorish castle, and halted about mid-day on the banks of the Elmonte.—Headquarters at Iaracejo.

Marshal Soult is again in Placentia, and his out-posts at Coria. Some British soldiers, who were left sick in that city, fell into his hands, but have since made their escape, and arrived at Zarza Major, where Marshal Beresford is at present, with the two brigades of infantry, under the command of Generals Lightburne, and Catlin Crawford. Sir R. Wilson has retired into Portugal, after a severe action with part of Ney's corps, near the Pass of Banos. The French have their piquets on the right bank of the Tagus, opposite to Almaraz, where General Robert Crawford is stationed with a division in advance.

His men bathe in the river, and exchange civilities with the enemy, without receiving the smallest molestation.

Cuesta has thought proper to resign the command of his army, and is succeeded by General Eguia.

By the courtesy of Marshal Mortier, who commands at Talavera, accounts have been received of the wounded. He has placed sentries over the quarters of the officers and hospitals, to prevent any of their property being pillaged, and has advanced money to some out of his own pocket.

LETTER XX.

Truxillo.—Tomb of Pizarro, &c.

Truxillo, 20th of August, 1809.

This morning, soon after day-break, the 1st and 4th divisions of the army quitted the valley d'Elmonte, in which they had halted since the 11th instant, and after a march of 4 leagues, reached Truxillo, close to which, the troops *bivouaced* for the night.

Truxillo was formerly a town of some note, but is now only famous for having been the birth-place of Pizarro, at whose house, in the square, the commander of the forces fixed his head-quarters. In the church of Santa Anna stood the monument erected to his memory, which was entirely demolished by the French. Small pieces of agate, of which the warrior's tomb had been constructed, lay scattered about. Adjoining to the church is a deserted nunnery, and a little beyond, the ancient Moorish castle, now a heap of ruins.

Mr. Dillon of the Commissariat, who **was** taken prisoner by the French on the

27th ult. at **Casalegas,** and subsequently effected his exchange, arrived this day from Talavera. This gentleman brings pleasing accounts of the wounded, who receive the most humane treatment from the enemy. The British prisoners are allowed to have the first choice of all articles brought into the market; and in every possible way, their comfort and accommodation has been invariably attended to.

LETTER XXI.

Route of the British to Merida.—Short account of the Roman Antiquities in that City.

Merida, 30th of August, 1809.

On the 21st instant, the division marched 3 leagues to the village of Casas del Puerto de Santa Cruz.

August the 22d, to Mayadas, 4 leagues, sub Jove as usual.—On the following morning, the division arrived about noon on the banks of the Guadiana, and halted opposite Medellin, at the foot of a handsome bridge of twenty arches. This day's march was nearly 4 leagues. Two miles from the town is the field where a severe engagement was fought, in April last, betwixt the French army, under Marshal Victor, and the army of Estremadura, commanded by General Cuesta; in which, the latter sustained a signal defeat.

Medellin is a small town, with a fine Moorish castle on an eminence, rising abruptly from the banks of the river. The whole face of the country, from the valley d'Elmonte, was without wood, and the greater part uncultivated, so that it is difficult to conceive whence the numerous towns and villages in this district, drew their fuel and subsistence. But the same observation equally applies to the whole of Spain through which the army marched, very different in appearance from the fertile vallies, the rich corn fields, and vineyards of Portugal. The residence of a gentleman was no where to be seen, but in the towns: very few farm-houses, and here and there, only the solitary hut of a goatherd.

On the 24th, after a most fatiguing march of 6 leagues, under a burning sun, the division arrived in the city of Merida, and crossing the ancient Roman bridge of sixty arches, which was constructed by Augustus Cæsar, 28 years before Christ, the troops halted on the south bank of the Guadiana.

Merida was once a considerable Roman station, and there still exist many noble reliques of antiquity, in tolerable preservation. The gate of the temple of Mars, one of the first edifices to which the curiosity of a stranger, particularly if a military man, is directed, alone remains entire, and forms the entrance to a modern church. Under the inscription *Marti sacrum Vitella paculi*, is another, illustrative of its present designation.—*Iam non Marti sacrum sed Jesu Christo consecratum.*

At a short distance from the scite of the temple, three antique Roman altars, which were dug up about a century ago, are placed one above another, and form a handsome pedestal, surmounted by the statue of a Spanish king.

The area of the temple of Diana is now filled by a modern building; but the columns, with most of their capitals, remain in a perfect state, and are built into the walls of the house, still, however, in such a way, as to leave them fully exposed to view. One window of exquisite beauty, has been carefully preserved.

The superb aqueduct, built by the Romans, is now in ruins; but several arches are still standing, and convey to the mind of a spectator, a tolerably just conception of its former magnificence.

Beyond the present extent of Merida, are two amphitheatres; the largest of which is supposed to have been the Naumachia. It seems more probable, however, that the exhibition of sea fights must have taken place on an island near the bridge, where are the remains of some considerable works. The lesser amphitheatre has been converted by the Spaniards, into a *Plaza de Toros*, for which purpose, the arena is now enclosed.

In front of the Corregidor's house, in the square, are seven beautiful columns of white marble, supposed to have belonged to a Roman temple. In a street, a little beyond, is an arch of prodigious magnitude, which originally formed one of the entrances of the city, and was, probably, a memorial of some great victory. Amongst the ruins of an old house, prostrate on the ground, and neglected, lay a colossal statue of Diana, as a vestal: the head and arms were gone, but the drapery of the figure was remarkably fine, and bespoke the merit of the artist. In the principal court of the ancient Moorish castle, is the bath of Diana, to which the descent is by a passage of 50 steps. A most beautiful pilastre of the composite order, was placed at the entrance.

A little beyond the castle, are the remains of some buildings, which, from their situation and appearance, are conjectured to have been the public baths of the Romans.

About a mile from the city and near to the modern aqueduct, is the circus where the chariot races were held. By the situation of the Roman gate, under which, the high road from Madrid passes, and the ruins of the walls, an idea may be formed of the ancient boundaries of this city, which must have been of great extent. Indeed, tradition says, that Merida contained 150,000 inhabitants.

After the battle of Medellin, a small French force had possession of the castle for some weeks, and barricaded the bridge, to prevent the passage of a Spanish corps which was posted on the opposite bank of the Guadiana. At length, the Spaniards forced their way under the fire of a few guns which the enemy had mounted, and passed through the city to a height, commanding the castle which they were preparing to cannonade, when a considerable body of French cavalry made their appearance. The Spaniards conceiving them to be the advance of Victor's army, retired with precipitation, which gave the garrison an opportunity to make good their retreat unmolested, being covered by the cavalry.

LETTER XXII.

The 1st division of the British encamp on the Banks of the Guadiana.—Positions of the French.

Talavera de Real, 27th September, 1809.

At day-break, on the 2d instant, General Sherbrooke's division moved off on the road to Badajos, and about 11 o'clock, halted within 2 miles of the village of Lobon.

Next day the troops advanced at the same early hour, and after a march of 2 leagues, constructed huts, on a plain watered by the Guadiana, about half a league from the inconsiderable town of Talavera la Real, and 4 from Badajos, where head-quarters were established.

The following are understood to be the present positions of the French corps :—

Victor's division is betwixt Talavera de la Reyna and La Mancha; Sebastiani, who was wounded on the 28th of July, is in La Mancha; Mortier at Oropesa; Arzobispo, and Naval Moral, and Marshal Ney, after his engagement with Sir Robert Wilson, returned to Salamanca.

On the 13th, Lord Blantyre arrived with the 2d battalion of the 42d regiment, to join General Cameron's brigade; and on the following day, General Catlin Crawford's brigade, consisting of the 2d battalions of the 28th, Honorable Lieutenant-Colonel Abercrombie; 34th, Lieutenant-Colonel Maister, and 39th, Lieutenant-Colonel Wilson, forded the river at this place, on their route to join Lieutenant-General Hill's division at Montejo, Puebla Nova and Torremayor.

This morning a troop of horse artillery marched to relieve Captain Ross's troop at Merida; the latter having lost a great number of horses in the retreat from Talavera.

Preparations are now making for the removal of the guards into Badajos, which the brigade anticipate with much satisfaction, having been constantly in the field since the latter end of June.

The army has become very sickly. This is considered the most unhealthy time of the year, but the approaching rainy season is expected to clear the air and dispel the pestilential fever, so fatal to the troops. The Guadiana, at this period, is reckoned so unwholesome, that the Spaniards will not use the water, or eat of the fish taken in it. Another reason assigned for this repugnance, is, that after the battle of Medellin, a considerable number of the slain were thrown into the river.

The Marquis of Romana having taken his seat at Seville, as one of the supreme Junta, is succeeded by the Duke del Parque in the command of his army. Head-quarters at Ciudad Rodrigo. The Duke of Albuquerque, with about 10,000 men, is stationed in front, beyond Merida; and General Eguia has proceeded to join Venegas in La Mancha, with the remainder of Cuesta's army, upwards of 20,000 men.

LETTER XXIII.

The Guards go into Cantonments in Badajos.—Lieutenant-General Sherbrooke receives the Order of the 'Bath.—Viscount Wellington's Gala.

Badajos, 15th October, 1809.

THE Guards quitted their encampment of huts on the 9th of October, and marched into quarters at Talavera la Real. At the same time, General Cameron's brigade took the road to Lobon. Next morning, the guards resumed their march, and about noon, arrived in the city of Badajos, the capital of the province of Estremadura. The Officers were quartered upon the inhabitants, and the men in convents.

Badajos contains 6 monasteries, the same number of nunneries, and a population of 7 to 8000. The fortifications are partly ancient, partly modern: the fine Roman bridge over the Guadiana, is defended by a *tete de pout,* on which, a few guns are mounted. On the right bank of the river, stands the fort of St. Christoval, which commands the city. Badajos was twice besieged by the Portuguese, but never taken.

On the 7th instant, the commander of the forces gave an entertainment upon the occasion of Lieutenant-General Sherbrooke being invested with the insignia of the Bath. Immediately after the ceremony, a royal salute was fired. About 8 o'clock the nobility and principal inhabitants of Badajos began to assemble at Lord Wellington's, and after a few songs from the ladies, the ball was opened with an English country dance, by a General Officer and Donna Anna Fortunata, of Elvas. The dancing continued until midnight, when supper was announced. The party broke up about 2 o'clock.

LETTER XXIV.

Birth-Day of Ferdinand VII.—The Public Promenade of Badajos, Tertullia.—Remarks.—Situation of the French Corps.

Badajos, 29th October, 1809.

THE 14th instant being the birth-day of Ferdinand, a royal salute was fired from the ramparts.

In the afternoon there was a numerous assemblage on the Almada, the public promenade, or prado of this city, near the river, where the inhabitants, of all ranks, are accustomed to take the air. Several beautiful women were present, who attracted attention by their engaging, yet not immodest looks, and the graceful ease of their carriage. The veil, which is universally worn, no longer serves to conceal their faces, and the *toute ensemble* of their simple and elegant dress, is admirably adapted to display a fine form to the best advantage.

A short religious ceremony, peculiar to this nation, is deserving of notice. At sunset, every evening, the bells of the convents and churches are tolled for a few moments. On hearing this signal, the people cease conversing with each other and quit their occupations, and all in silence, address a short prayer to the protecting power, which has brought them in safety to the close of another day.

There are no public places of amusement in Badajos; but one Lady Donna Payna, opens her house every night to the best society and the British Officers, who are received with the utmost politeness. Conversation, cards, the song and dance, succeed each other, and form what is called the tertullia, similar in most respects to a London route.

On the above evening, the tertullia was particularly well attended. The young and lovely Marchioness D'Almeida and the handsome widow Donna Manuela, were the admired and principal ornaments of the assembly. There were several other ladies present, who maintained the reputation of their country for the beauty of its women. In general, the Spanish ladies are elegantly formed, and spare no pains in the decoration of their persons. They are remarkably mild and engaging in their manner and address, but few of them speak any language except their own, and the education of all is extremely confined. A Spanish lover is certain of seeing his mistress, at least, once a day, as nothing but indisposition prevents all classes from attending church. The Duenna still forms part of the establishment of a Spanish household, but without her former authority and privileges. Ladies of a certain rank, never stir abroad without a female attendant, who, if they are young, is about their own age, and more a companion disposed to promote their wishes, than a rigid observer of their actions.

About 10 o'clock, the commander of the forces and part of his staff arrived. The widow Donna Manuela, accompanied on the guitar by Senhor Fuentes, sung a Spanish ballad in a pleasing style, and with much taste. A country dance was afterwards formed; at the end of which, Donna Josepha Basquez danced a bolera, playing the castanets at the same time, in a most graceful manner. The same young lady and Donna

Payna, in the course of the evening, entertained the company with their favourite national dance, the Fandango.

The Spanish gentlemen have a natural reserve, and an appearance of *hauteur* about them, which, at first sight, is calculated to displease. They have for some years past, adopted the French mode of dress, and the Portuguese have followed their example in this respect. They are remarkably temperate in their manner of living, although, on particular occasions, they indulge in drinking hot-spiced wines to excess. It is the fashion to dine at an early hour, and all ranks afterwards take the *siesta*, at which time, the houses and shops are shut up, and the most populous city, during this part of the afternoon, appears to be quite deserted and wrapt in the silence of the grave. This is one reason, perhaps, why the British have not been admitted to their tables, as they may not chuse, out of compliment to any foreigners, to forego their national customs.

On the 21st, 2 privates of the guards arrived, who made their escape from Madrid on the 15th ult. They report, that above 20

British Officers, taken at Talavera, marched on the 10th for France. The prisoners uniformly receive the most humane treatment from the enemy.

On the 1st of September, Marshal Ney was at Salamanca, with 14,000 men; Soult at Placentia, Zarza Major, and Coria, with 8000; Victor's head-quarters at Oropesa and 4000; Marshal Mortier at Talavera, with 10,000 men, and General Sebastiani is said to be in motion to the South, with a division of nearly the same strength.

The Honourable Captain Alexander Gordon, who went with a flag of truce to the French out-posts, has brought intelligence of Austria having made peace with France.

Beside the brigade of Guards, the 1st battalion of the 40th, and 3d of the 27th regiments, are quartered in Badajos. The duties of the fortress are taken by the Spanish troops.

LETTER XXV.

Escape of two British Officers from Madrid, &c.

Badajos, 29th November, 1809.

Two officers of the 61st regiment, who had been wounded and taken prisoners at Talavera, arrived here on the 9th instant, having escaped from the convent in which they were confined at Madrid. They remained concealed in that city for 8 days, and on their way hither, passed through the Spanish army in La Mancha. General Ariezaga had his head-quarters at Damiel; Colonel Roche and Lord Macduff were with him. From the proximity of the enemy, a battle may be expected soon to take place, but the Spanish leader has it in his power to avoid an engagement.

On the 12th instant the Commander of the forces returned from Cadiz, where the Marquis Wellesley has embarked on his return to England.

Lieutenant-General Sir Stapleton Cotton remains at Merida, with the principal part of the British cavalry. General Hill's division of infantry at Montego, Puebla, &c. The light infantry under Brigadier-General Robert Crawford at Campo Mayor. Major-General Cole at Olivenza, and Brigadier-General Cameron at Lobon and Almondarelehy.

The Spaniards under Lieutenant-General Don Luis Bassecourt, occupy a line betwixt Merida and the Tagus. Head-quarters at Truxillo.

LETTER XXVI.

Remarks on some of the leading features of the Campaign.—In consequence of the Army of La Mancha under General Ariezaga being defeated, the British break up from Spain.—Route of the first division.—The Guards at the head of the column reach Abrantes, passing through the following places on their march.— Elvas.— Barbacena.— Montforte.— Portalegre. — Gafete and Gavio.—Sick left at Abrantes.

Abrantes, 16*th December,* 1809.

THE events which followed the ever memorable battle of Talavera, so glorious to the British arms, and which at first seemed to promise the greatest advantages to the cause of the peninsula, have been already detailed in the preceding letters.

In reviewing these events, a variety of reflections naturally present themselves, and the mind sickens at the melancholy consequences of the imbecility of those chiefs, to whose guidance the Spanish armies were entrusted; who by their futile plans conceived without judgment, and attempted to be carried into execution without ability, disappointed alike the hopes of their country and the British leader, who in vain looked forward to any co-operation which might produce a beneficial result to the general cause.

On Sir Arthur Wellesley marching from Talavera with the avowed intention of attacking Marshal Soult at Placentia, Cuesta ought to have moved forward with his army, and taken post on the right bank of the Alberche, with one corps passed over that river, and strong piquets of cavalry to watch the enemy. The effect of this movement on the operations of the British must be obvious ; and it will not be doubted by military men, that had Cuesta assumed this attitude, which would have enabled him to intercept all communication betwixt the French armies, and maintained his position as agreed upon, the Commander of the forces would have been again successful in a rencontre with the French who had arrived at Placentia, although their number was upwards of 50,000, composed of the remains of Marshal Soult's division which had escaped from Oporto, with those of Ney and Mortier. The British troops were flushed with victory, they placed an entire confidence in their general, and were to be opposed to the corps of the same enemy

K

whom they had recently defeated in the most signal manner. There were other circumstances also highly favourable to the British continuing to act on a system of offensive warfare; the army had been reinforced by the addition of General Robert Crawford's fine brigade of light infantry, and a troop of horse artillery. Marshal Beresford was on the frontier, threatening the enemy's rear, whilst that active and enterprising officer, Sir Robert Wilson, made a rapid march across the mountains and alarmed his left.

This was the state of affairs, when the British army, by the unexpected march of General Cuesta from Talavera, was compelled to retire to the left bank of the Tagus, followed by the Spanish troops. A considerable number of the latter withdrew into the mountains of La Mancha, where, if unable to offer any obstacle to the progress of the French, they were at least, in a state of immediate security and daily acquiring numbers. Meanwhile, the British fell back upon the frontier, and occupied the line of the Guadiana, the advance being at Merida. At the same time, that the troops were easily subsisted in this

quainted with his opinion of the real sentiments of the people, the capacity of their rulers, and the numbers and discipline of their armies.

By such or similar motives, the Commander of the forces appears to have been actuated. The low flat plains of Spanish Estramadura, and nearly the whole of the country watered by the Guadiana, have been noticed by different writers as the most unhealthy part of the peninsula. The British troops were, unhappily, destined to prove the truth of this remark, and numbers of the brave fellows, whose constitutions had borne up against all the fatigues and privations of the campaign, sunk under the baneful influence of this destructive climate. The state of inaction, in which the troops now remained, proved too sudden a change after their extraordinary exertions, during the retreat from Talavera, and was, doubtless, another cause of the sickness which spread rapidly throughout the army, to counteract which, orders were given, that they should be frequently exercised in short marches, whenever the weather permitted. The end of autumn, and the latter

position, the safety of the province of Andalusia was ensured, as the enemy could not attempt to penetrate into the Sierra Morena, with the British army on his right flank. In other respects, however, the position was not an eligible one, and it may be fairly presumed, that the Commander of the forces went into cantonments on the Guadiana, for the purposes of giving confidence to the army of La Mancha, and of encouraging the people to persevere in the cause, but more particularly to afford the Spanish nation an opportunity of reforming its government, and of choosing new men to direct their measures in the cabinet, and conduct their armies in the field. The arrival of the Marquis Wellesley, whose abilities and experience might naturally be **expected,** not only to aid such a reform, but to point out to the Spaniards, those measures which ought to be adopted, to call forth the military and financial resources of the country, to administer them with judgment and prudence, was another circumstance which might have had considerable weight in deciding on the necessity of remaining in Spain, until the government of England should be ac-

part of a campaign, produce the same effects in all armies; besides, it was observed, that the prevalence of malignant fevers was greater at this period, both in Spain and Portugal, than had been known for several preceding years.

The communication with Lisbon, by either bank of the Tagus, continued uninterrupted; indeed, the enemy evinced no disposition to make any movement towards the quarter in which the British army was stationed.

The Marquis of Romana was at Seville, where he had taken his seat as one of the Supreme Junta, but even the accession of his councils, dictated as they were by talent and undoubted patriotism, failed to inspire a confidence of this government in the minds of the people, and those measures, which were alone calculated to rouse the energies of the Spaniards in the cause of liberty, and direct their efforts with the happiest effect, still remained untried.

A sudden and fatal blow was now about to be struck, and the genius of freedom seemed overwhelmed by the dire calamity.

The army of La Mancha, to the chief command of which, Lieutenant General Don Juan de Ariesaga had been appointed, was highly respectable, both in numbers and the component parts of which it was formed. A plan of operations was said to have been drawn up and submited to this general by the Baron de Croisard, an intelligent officer and Commissioner from the Emperor of Austria to the Spanish armies. Whether this plan, which had for its object to drive the French out of Madrid, and beyond the Banks of the Ebro, by a series of manœuvres, without risking a battle, would have been successful or not, it is impossible to say, as the Spanish chief did not think proper to adopt it; but contrary to the wishes and opinion of all around him, and to every principle of prudence or of military tactics, General Ariesaga, in an unhappy moment, blindly resolved to quit the mountains, and descending into the plains to commit himself with new formed levies against the veteran troops of France. The whole South of Spain, by the dispersion of Ariesagas' army after the unfortunate battle of Ocana, lay open to the incursions of the enemy, and it became no longer necessary or desirable in a military point of view, to retain the British army on the borders of Estramadura. At 8 on the morning of the 8th instant, the guards marched from Badajos with a brigade of heavy six-pounders, under the command of Captain Lawson, followed on successive days by the King's German legion and General Cameron's brigade.

The preceding day was the festival of the Virgin, which is always kept with much religious pomp and ceremony by the Spaniards. High mass was celebrated in the cathedral, which is of Moorish architecture, the interior hung entirely with crimson velvet and gold. The ceremony, at all times solemn and impressive, was interrupted by the sudden fainting of one of the officiating canons, a venerable priest, 85 years of age. On being carried into the open air, he recovered.—Several salutes in honor of the saint were fired from the ramparts, and in the evening the principal inhabitants assembled in their best attire on the Almada.

At the distance of a league from Badajos, on the road to Elvas, the brigade forded a small river, the Caya, which in its course to the Guadiana, forms the boundary of the two kingdoms, and re-entered Portugal after an absence of five months. A little after mid-day the guards reached Elvas, which at the time was the principal depôt of the sick and wounded. This city, seated on a hill, is one of the strongest places in Portugal. On an eminence stands the celebrated fort built by General Count la Lippe, and called after his name. A very noble aqueduct supplies Elvas with water.

On the 10th, to Barbacena, two long leagues over a heath, cloathed with gum schistus, myrtle and rosemary, and here and there a clump of olive trees.—The day remarkably cold, with a thick haze. At 1 the 3d guards arrived in the village.

On the 11th to Montforte, the same distance as yesterday; the country through which the road lay was extremely picturesque and well wooded. Montforte is a town of some note, with an ancient castle now in ruins. Here is a monastery and nunnery, the latter dedicated to Santa Francisca. The nuns who appeared at the grate were more agreeable and lively in their manners than is usually found in the recluse inhabitants of a convent.

December the 12th, to Portalegre 20 miles; the face of the country extremely beautiful, the greater part a forest of fine oak, cork and pine trees. This city is the see of a bishop, and contains two monasteries, three nunneries, and about 5000 inhabitants; it is romantically situated on a hill, and the surrounding country appears well cultivated. Here the brigade re-united, the Coldstream having proceeded from Elvas by a different route, through the towns of San Olaia and Assumar on the right.

Halted on the 13th, which allowed the officers an opportunity of visiting the bishop's palace and cathedral; the latter a very noble modern pile.

On the following day the brigade marched by Apalhao to Gafeté, 16 miles. Soon after leaving the beautiful environs of Portalegre, the column entered on a wild uncultivated district, and about 4 o'clock halted in this miserable place. The road throughout was rugged, and the guns in front could only proceed slowly, which obstructed the march of the troops. There not being sufficient accommodation in Cafeté, the light infantry and artillery went forward to the small town of Toloza.

Yesterday the guards reached Gavio, about 3 in the afternoon, having marched 4 leagues through a country similar in appearance to that over which the troops had passed on the preceding day, until they approached the banks of the Tagus, when the scenery became at once bold and picturesque.

The road this morning led the whole distance 18 miles, through a beautiful district, in a line with the course of the Tagus. The appearance of the castle of Abrantes from the south bank of the river had an imposing air of grandeur. About 3 P.M. the brigade crossed the bridge of boats, and ascended the eminence on which the town stands, in the midst of a fertile country.

During the whole of the march from Elvas, the troops were cheerfully supplied by the inhabitants with whatever they had for sale, at a moderate rate ; they often expressed their fears that the British were upon the point of withdrawing from Portugal. Guides were provided at each stage on the route.

LETTER XXVII.

March of the Guards to Leyria, &c.

Leyria, 29th December, 1809.

On the 17th instant the brigade halted in Abrantes, where the sick of the army were embarked on the Tagus for Lisbon.

The naturally strong situation of the town, (which must be considered the key of the Tagus,) is improving by works constructed under the direction of the royal engineers. A considerable magazine had been formed here during the time the British were in Spain.

The stormy and boisterous night of the 17th was succeeded by a lovely morning; and the guards again bent their way to Punhete, over the vale of Abrantes, which is esteemed the granary of Portugal. The orange-trees tinted with the yellow foliage of autumn, and bending beneath the weight of their golden fruit, gave a richness to the scenery which vied with the beauties of summer. Soon after mid-day the brigade arrived in the village, and occupied their former cantonments. The inhabitants received them with kindness, and expressed their deep regret for the fate of those who had fallen in the battle of Talavera.

On the following day the guards continued their march, and about 2 o'clock in the afternoon reached Thomar. The brigade was again quartered in the convent of Christ.

Marshal Beresford has his head quarters in this city, and General Miranda is also here, with two brigades of infantry.

Yesterday the guards arrived in Leyria about 3 in the afternoon, having halted on the preceding night at Ourem. The roads from Punhete were rendered very bad by the late rains.

Brigadier-General Coleman commands the garrison, which consists of about 3000 Portuguese infantry.

LETTER XXVIII.

The Guards arrive at Vizeu.—Short Account of that ancient City.

Vizeu, 31st December, 1809.

YESTERDAY the brigade of guards which led the column during the march of the British army through Portugal, arrived in this city.

On the 22d instant the guards left Leyria, and passing through the towns of Pombal and Condiexa, entered Coimbra on Christmas Day. Their reception in that city was friendly and hospitable, although not distinguished with the same lively expressions of gratitude as the inhabitants evinced on their first visit, when the British came to deliver them from an enemy whose approach they had for some time awaited with the utmost apprehension.

Coimbra wore a more gay and busy appearance than formerly. A number of families who had fled from their homes were returned; the restoration of quiet by the expulsion of Marshal Soult's army had admitted of the University being re-opened, and the youth of Portugal were once more pursuing their studies. The academic dress was uniform and simple, yet extremely becoming.

The gardens of Santa Cruz even at this advanced season of the year, were still delightful; the way to them was through the dormitory of the convent, from which a path led to the quinta or country house, seated in an orange grove, where the holy brethren of St. Augustine occasionally retired to relax their minds from the severity of monastic duties. The appearance of every thing about the quinta bespoke wealth and comfort; a suite of apartments terminating with a billiard-room, opened to a terrace from which there was a charming view over the extensive gardens. The cellars were filled with the produce of their own vineyards.—During the first stay of the army in this city, a table was kept for the officers at Santa Cruz, and a handsome entertainment daily provided.

Next day, the 26th, being a festival, was celebrated with much splendor in the nunnery of St. Clare. On this occasion the magnificent tomb of the foundress Queen Isabella, was decorated with a profusion of jewels and flowers, through which a small rill of water was seen to flow. At noon the Lady Superior, attired in the robes of the order, her train borne by the two eldest nuns, entered the chapel, and passing with a slow and solemn step to a seat at the upper end, around which the nuns were already ranged, a beautiful girl in the habit of a novice, who sat at the organ, commenced the symphony, after which the anthem was sung in full chorus by the sisterhood. The voice of Maria ———, the young and interesting votary of St. Clare, within whose holy walls she had fled for refuge on the first invasion of Portugal by the French, was distinguished above the rest by its sweetness and variety of tone. Charmed with the manners of its inhabitants, and the peaceful solitudes of a cloister, Maria ———, at the early age of 17, after passing through a short noviciate, voluntarily embraced the veil. A bewitching grace sat upon the fair and polished forehead of the young *religieuse*, and the mild yet touching expression of her lovely countenance indicated the purity of her mind.

After high mass the Lady Abbess and several of the nuns approached the grate and welcomed the officers again to Coimbra.

On the 27th the brigade advanced to Malheada, 13 miles; and on the 28th to Martigoa, 4 leagues. The route lay over the steep and rugged mountain of Busaco, on whose summit the towers of a convent of the order of La Trappe, appeared to rise out of a beautiful wood. The extensive grounds were inclosed within a lofty wall; and it is scarcely possible to conceive a more sequestered spot than the scite of this monastery.

Descending the mountain, the troops entered a well-cultivated valley, and about 3 o'clock arrived in the village, where the 3d regiment was with difficulty accommodated. The Coldstream proceeded to a hamlet, a league beyond.

On the 29th to Tondella, 4 leagues; this little town is situated in a beautiful district. Next day, after a march of 15 miles, the guards reached this city; the Coldstream occupied the Bishop's Palace; the 3d guards the Convents of St. Antonio, and the Congregation of Oratory.

Vizeu situated in the centre of the province of Beira, betwixt the Mondego and the Vouga, is an episcopal city, and of great antiquity. The inhabitants indeed pretend that it was founded by the Turduli, a Gothic race, 500 years before Christ, and originally named Vacca ; but to support this they produce no satisfactory document. The account which is considered as most entitled to credit is, that this city was built in the time of Sertorius by the pro-consul D. Brutus, who called it Vicontium. Two towers adjoining the cathedral yet remain, of Roman construction, on which appear the eagle, and the names of Flaccus and Frontinius, who are supposed to have been the architects. Northward of the city is a Roman camp of considerable magnitude, in which the hitherto victorious legions of Rome were compelled to remain inactive before the town, by the renowned Portuguese general Viriatus, whose memory is held in repute by his countrymen to this day. A small village, Alvoka, in the

Sierra de Estrella, is pointed out as the birth-place of this leader, who from being originally a captain of banditti, was chosen to command the Lusitanian army, and became the terror of the Romans.

Vizeu contains two monasteries, a convent for nuns, and about 5000 inhabitants. There is a good weekly market, and the surrounding country is well cultivated.—The peasantry in this district are of a more industrious character than those of the south.

The Benedictines seemed to partake in the general satisfaction excited by the arrival of the British; and refreshments were presented to the officers who visited the grate. All the confectionary is made in the convents, and this forms one source of the revenue of these institutions. The nuns of Vizeu were more unreserved in their manners than one would expect from the secluded life they lead, and the nature of their establishment. They were sufficiently talkative, and old and young had a wonderful share of curiosity to know what was passing in the world.

The bishop is 70 years of age, and resides principally at a quinta, a short distance from the city. Some of the officers went to pay their respects, and found him dining upon a single dish; his chaplains seated at another table, were also partaking of a very frugal repast—this was a little after mid-day. The bishop politely rose on their entrance, and hastened to express his extreme gratification at seeing a British army in his diocese.

With the exception of the 1st division, the whole of the army proceeded to the frontier by the route of St. Combadao, after passing through Coimbra.

LETTER XXIX.

The British Army in Winter Quarters.—Marshal Ney summons Ciudad Rodrigo, and Victor overrunning the Province of Andalusia suddenly appears before Cadiz, to which place the Honourable General W. Stewart was dispatched from Lisbon, with a Brigade of Infantry.—Skirmish at the Out-posts.

Vizeu, 20th February, 1810.

EARLY in January, the whole of the British army had arrived in their new position, and the troops were quietly settled in winter quarters. The Commander of the forces after a short visit to Lisbon, for the purpose of reconnoitreing the chain of works constructing in its vicinity, had returned to this city, in front of which, the main body of his infantry was cantoned in the several towns and villages on the road to the frontier, with the exception of the 2d division, and Major-General Slade's brigade of cavalry, which continued on the line of the Tagus, under the command of Lieutenant-General Hill.

The out-posts were stationed on the Banks of the Coa, and the duty taken by the light brigade, and 1st German hussars, under the orders of Brigadier-General Robert Crawford. The 3d division, Major-General Picton's, was the next in advance, supported by the 4th division, Major-General Cole's at Guarda, Celerico, and the villages in the valley of the Mondego; General Fane's brigade of heavy cavalry was in Coimbra, and the 16th light dragoons at St. Combadao.

The first 6 weeks succeeding the return of the British to Portugal, were passed in a state of comparative tranquillity; but within the last, a considerable sensation has been excited by the movements and demonstrations of the enemy in various parts of the peninsula.

On the 11th instant, the French, to the number of 9 or 10,000 approached Ciudad Rodrigo at 4 different points. At half-past 7 in the morning, a flag of truce arrived, with a letter from Marshal Ney, requiring the surrender of this fortress.—The governor, Don André de Herrasti returned a spirited refusal.

On the following day the enemy bombarded the city for several hours, without making any impression. Disappointed in his hope of entering Ciudad Rodrigo without resistance, Marshal Ney pushed his corps down to the river Aqueda, which he crossed at the bridge of San Felices, but finding it impracticable to bring his artillery over this pass, he withdrew his troops, and has cantoned them in the villages betwixt Ciudad Rodrigo and Salamanca, leaving a small corps of observation on the Aqueda.

Victor has arrived at Port St. Mary's, opposite Cadiz, and is in possession of Seville, and the immense magazines collected by the late Junta in that city, which he entered without opposition, in the same manner as he did at Jaen, Cordova and Granada, on his march to the south. Meanwhile, the remains of the army of La Mancha retired on Algeziras, and the Duke of Albuquerque entered Cadiz, with about 10,000 men, only 12 hours before Victor appeared. General William Stewart, who had been detached from Lisbon with a brigade of infantry, has also reached Cadiz, so that no fears are now entertained for the safety of that valuable place.

Joseph Buonaparte is with Victor's army.— The French have prevailed on a few of the prisoners taken at Ocana, to swear allegiance to him; and the discouraging aspect of affairs, induces many of the armed peasantry to return to their homes; but it is a war of partizans, the peasant against the soldier, and unless Joseph can keep a force in every town, he will not, for a long time, be enabled to subdue the spirit of the people. The most melancholy feature in the cause of Spain is, that most of the soldiers, when routed or dispersed, throw away their arms.

Last month, a French corps of 10,000 men, of which 2000 were cavalry, passed through Vittoria to Burgos, and then struck off on the road to Madrid. The cavalry appeared good troops, the infantry chiefly conscripts.

A smart skirmish took place on the 16th instant at the out-posts. The enemy after dusk, having passed a body of 600 men over the Aqueda, was opposed by 4 companies of the 95th regiment, under Lieutenant Colonel Beckwith, who compelled them to retire with a loss of 50 in killed, wounded and prisoners.—On the side of the British, Lieutenant Mercer and 12 men were killed.

LETTER XXX.

Description of the Country round Vizeu.—Festival of St. Josephine.

Vizeu, 1st March, 1810.

THE weather, which was unusually severe during the months of January and February has now become extremely mild, and the face of the country in the neighbourhood of this city, appears to great advantage. In every direction are beautiful walks and rides.

At the distance of a league is a remarkable hot spring on the banks of the Dao, a mountain torrent, which forces its way through rocks, in a valley of the most picturesque appearance.

The garden at the bishop's country house is a delightful spot, but it yields in point of beauty to the quinta of Don Jose Ernesto, about a mile from Vizeu. The road to it leads through an avenue of cherry trees already in blossom, to the Val de Besteros or Valley of Cattle, at the head of which, the house and grounds are situated. At each step the scenery becomes more romantic, and is uncommonly rich in all its features. The vale is bounded by a chain of hills, the Sierras de Caramula, whose summits at this moment are covered with snow.

But the grate of the Benedictine nunnery possessed more charms for the British officers than all the beauties of the surrounding district.—A regard for the eternal welfare of the nuns had induced the venerable bishop to express his displeasure to the Lady Abbess at their frequent visits; but this interference on the part of his reverence, was not attended with any visible effect.

Yesterday the church of the convent was filled at an early hour, it being the festival of their saint, whose image was adorned with jewels, a number of wax tapers burning before it, and the grand altar lighted up and embellished in a similar manner. The service of the day commenced, and all in silence listened to the sweet voices of the nuns, at times interrupted by the hollow tones of the officiating monks, who were celebrating high mass at the altar.—Again the harmony of the choir broke upon the ear, accompanied by the loud swell of the organ; and after a short pause, Sister *Joanna Perpetuza* sung a solo in a deep and powerful, yet melodious strain.—She was followed by *Maria Benedita*, who acquitted herself with much taste and execution in a difficult hymn. At this moment, a friar of the order of St. Francis entered the church, and kneeling on the steps of the altar, prayed for a short time; after which, he ascended the pulpit and delivered a sermon extempore.—When his discourse, which did not seem to make much impression upon the auditory, was ended, an anthem was chaunted by the whole of the nuns in full chorus.—Donna *Antonia Maria*, the fair novice of St. Josephine, played on the organ with a masterly hand.

LETTER XXXI.

Situation of the French Corps—Remarks on the War in the Peninsula.—General Robert Crawford throws himself into Fort Conception.

Vizeu, 14*th March,* 1810.

THE corps of the enemy are gathering fast around this kingdom, and form a cordon from Corunna to Cadiz. According to recent information, Junot is at St. Jago (betwixt Corunna and Vigo) and Marshal Ney continues on the right bank of the Aqueda, betwixt Ciudad Rodrigo and the bridges of Zamora and Ledesma, with his out-posts at San Felices, three leagues from the advance of Lord Wellington's army at Almeida.

On the other side of the Sierra de Francia, Marshal Soult is stationed, with his head-quarters at Placentia, securing with his right the important pass of Banos.

Mortier is at Talavera la Real, and his corps is cantoned in that town and the neighbouring ones, Almondarelehy, Zafra, Valverde and Olivenza.

The enemy are said to be strengthening Burgos, and there are 5 to 6000 men in that city, and about the same number in Valladolid. At Burgos, the French issued a proclamation offering pardon to such armed peasants of the guerilla (sharpshooters) as should return to their homes.

These detached corps of mounted peasants had cut off an escort near Vittoria, of 300 French bullocks going to the army, and put all the party to death. There is also an armed force of this description which hovers round Madrid and annoys the enemy's convoys.

There are occasional reports of large reinforcements to the French army passing through Bayonne, but every thing remains quiet upon the frontier, and the enemy has not renewed his attempt on Ciudad Rodrigo. This calm, however, may be the forerunner of a storm, for the designs of Buonaparte against the independence of the peninsula, are of a nature not to be doubted. The patriotism of the Spaniards, although chilled and repressed by the imbecility of their government and the gigantic efforts of Great Britain in defence of an injured and insulted nation have hitherto foiled the plans, and blasted the hopes of the usurper; but now that he can give his undivided attention to an object of so much importance as annexing the resources of this immense territory to the power of France, by placing the crown of Spain securely on his brother's head, it is impossible not to feel considerable anxiety for the ultimate result of this great contest.

Within these few days, General Robert Crawford has passed the frontier with the light division and a troop of horse artillery, and thrown himself into Fort Conception, two miles beyond Almeida. — Deserters, chiefly Germans, frequently come over, but from them little information can be obtained.

The sick of the army are sent every Monday to Fozdao, where they embark on the Mondego for Figueira, and from thence proceed to Lisbon.

LETTER XXXII.

The French are making Preparations for the Siege of Ciudad Rodrigo, &c.

Vizeu, 24th April, 1810.

ON the 22d ultimo, Mórtier's head quarters were at Zafra, with 9000 men, and Merlé at Meridia with 3 to 4000, having his outposts at Torremayor, &c. The whole of the enemy's force in Estramadura, does not exceed 15,000 men. Romana is at Badajos, and Balasteros, with the right of his army at Olivenza, where the French were for some time; the left extends to Albuquerque, and there are some troops in Campo Mayor. The number of Spaniards bearing arms is about 15,000, and as many more in training. The French are supposed to have not more than 25,000 men to the southward of the Sierra Morena.

The 2d division of infantry is at present quartered in Portalegre. — Major-General Slade's brigade of cavalry at Apalhao and Abrantes. — Lieutenant-General Hill is in communication with Badajos, and his light troops are at Nisa and Villa Velha to observe the movements of the enemy, should Regnier attempt to push a corps along the left bank of the Tagus.

Brigadier-General Howarth, and another troop of horse artillery have arrived at Lisbon.

The force under Marshal Ney is said to be increased from 15 to 25,000 men: with him are Generals Loison, Laborde and the younger Kellerman. Forty of Ney's body guards deserted the other day.—Frequent skirmishes take place at the out-posts, in which the British are uniformly successful.

Colonel Trant has proceeded from Oporto with 3000 men to defend the strong Pass of Salamonde, should Junot endeavour to penetrate into Portugal by that route.

Head-quarters moved on the 14th instant to Cea, a small town on the acclivity of the Estrella, the largest mountain in Portugal, at the distance of 6 leagues from Vizeu. Upon its summit are two lakes, from the greater, two of the principal rivers in this kingdom, the Mondego and Zezere take their rise; the Alva derives its source from the lesser. The country is highly beautiful and romantic, and the green vallies at the foot of the Estrella, form a remarkable contrast with its snow covered sides.

On the 19th instant Lord Wellington returned to Vizeu.

This morning, two Spanish deputies arrived from Ciudad Rodrigo, to request the Commander of the forces would move up to the relief of that city, in the event of its being attacked, for which the French appeared to be making serious preparation.

LETTER XXXIII.

The British move up to the frontiers.—Head-quarters at Celerico. —Marshal Beresford at Fornos.—Astorga surrenders to Junot. —Massena arrives at Salamanca.—City of Guarda.

Celerico, 20th May, 1810.

About 1 o'clock on the morning of the 27th instant, an order was issued for the guards to advance, each man carrying 3 days provisions, and biscuit for six days on mules. Although this order was equally sudden and unexpected, yet the whole were in readiness at the appointed hour, and marched from Vizeu, with the good wishes of the inhabitants, to Mongualde, 2 leagues, where the brigade arrived soon after mid-day. The country on the right, was extremely beautiful and picturesque. The weather hazy, with frequent showers; Sir Stapleton Catton's head-quarters, were at the magnificent mansion of the Paez family. General Cameron's brigade, under the command of Lord Blantyre, marched from Mongualde this morning, and the whole of the army was in motion, to take up a position nearer the frontier. The Commander of the forces passed through to Celerico. The Coldstream went 2 leagues further to Villacova.

April the 28th, to Fornos, 3 leagues over a very hilly road. In these 2 last towns, the troops were but indifferently accommodated. The day was remarkably warm, and the beautiful green fields every where carefully cultivated, formed a striking contrast with the barren summit of the neighbouring Estrella.

On the 29th, the guards arrived at Celerico, which not affording sufficient quarters for the brigade, the Coldstream proceeded to Lagiosa, in the Val de Mondego, and 4 companies of the 3d regiment to the village of Frontilhera.

The Mondego, after running for some leagues due north, makes a bend round Celerico, and then pursues its course to the Atlantic, in a westerly direction. The antient name of this town, is said to have been Siliobrigum, and here are the remains of a Roman fort, but of its history, no certain information can be obtained from the inhabitants.

The clergy are almost the only class who possess any learning, and even among them a great number are extremely ignorant, and know little of their country. In this respect they differ from their neighbours, the Spaniards, who take a pride in the traditions handed down by their ancestors, and dwell with a peculiar delight on a recital of those battles, which ended in the total expulsion of the Moors. It is only from foreign authors, that the Portuguese can derive a just knowledge of their country, as their own historians give such a colouring to facts, as to leave little semblance to the truth.

Astorga, a town without walls, and garrisoned by 3000 men, has surrendered to Junot after a months siege, during which the French lost about 6000 men.

Ney has his position on the Tormes. His advance on the Agueda.

Regnier shewed himself before Badajoz, on the 12th inst. when he was fired at from the batteries.

A French officer came in this morning, who states, that he deserted in consequence of an affront offered to him by his commandant upon whom he drew his sword. He says that Massena is at Salamanca, that the French have been reinforced, and are now 80,000 strong betwixt that city and Ciudad Rodrigo.

Marshal Beresford's head-quarters are at Fornos, and several brigades of Portuguese infantry have arrived in this neighbourhood.

The advance under General R. Crawford, has fallen back upon Almeida, but 4 companies of the 45th regiment, and some Portuguese troops are in Fort Conception, and the cavalry patrole to the banks of the Agueda, close to which, and in sight opposite are the enemy's piquets, who as well as the British, try the fords daily. There is no doubt entertained in this army, that Massena intends to commence active operations as soon as the weather will permit, but the rains still continue. His force is stated, by all deserters, at not less than 70,000; this includes Junot's corps of 20,000 men, lately arrived from the north.

Regnier is still in Estremadura, but is expected to combine with Massena, in the attack on Portugal.

The French gain no ground in the good will of the Spaniards, and their influence does not extend beyond the range of their cannon. Buonaparte has lately issued a decree, directing the French generals, who command in Spain to levy contributions on the inhabitants, for the subsistence and payment of their armies, as they must not expect any more money for this purpose.

The ancient city of Guarda, at the distance of 2 leagues from hence, is situated on the northern extremity of the Estrella. After passing through the village of Lagiosa and the romantic scenery of the Val de Mondego, the road winds up a steep hill, from whence the city appears at the distance of a mile. Here are few objects worthy of notice. The cathedral, a rude gothic pile was built in the 11th century. The castle of a later date, is now in ruins, what time had spared, having been demolished by the French. From the walls a remarkable fine view is obtained of the country to Ciudad Rodrigo, in front of a range of hills ten leagues distant.

On the left appears Pinhel, and 3 leagues further, the fortress of Almeida, on the

Spanish side of the Coa, over which there is a stone bridge, 2 miles from the town.

The fine commanding plain of Guarda naturally points it out, as the station for a body of troops, to observe and check the incursion of a hostile force on this part of the frontier, and when pressed by superior numbers, it will be in the commander's option to fall back upon his reinforcements, by the roads on either side of the Estrella.

LETTER XXXIV.

Ciudad Rodrigo besieged and taken after a most gallant defence.— The British out-posts withdrawn to Val de Lamula, &c.

Celerico, 24th July, 1810.

ON the 25th of June, the Commander of the forces and the heads of military departments, moved from Celerico to Almeida; and on the 30th to Alverca, 3 leagues or midway betwixt this town and Almeida.

On the 17th the French having completed their trenches before Ciudad Rodrigo, invested the place with a force of 30,000 infantry and 5000 cavalry. Deserters say that the troops have only a quarter ration of biscuit without meat, and no forage for their horses.

On the night of the 25th of June the enemy opened his batteries against Ciudad Rodrigo, and after a most gallant defence, during which about 700 of the inhabitants were killed by the bombardment, the Governor, seeing no hopes of relief, and his provisions and ammunition being nearly exhausted, surrendered by capitulation on the evening of the 10th instant.

The Marquis of Romana came from Badajos for the purpose it was said of requesting Lord Wellington would advance to its relief, but departed perfectly satisfied with the propriety of the British leader's reasons for declining to make a forward movement; which, by endangering the safety of his army, might ultimately compromise the general cause.

On the 28th ultimo the enemy having driven in the British out-posts to Alomeda, 1 league beyond Fort Conception hutted at Gallegos with his advanced guard, and on the 5th instant his force having increased on this side of the Agueda, General Crawford withdrew his piquets into Fort Conception, which he abandoned on the 21st and the British out-posts retired to Val de Lamula. On that day a skirmish took place, in which Lieutenant-Colonel Talbot, of the 14th dragoons, was killed; the cavalry made 2 officers and 30 men prisoners, who declare that the French army is much straitened for provisions.

General Cameron's brigade moved forward to Minucal Baraçal and the adjacent villages, a league in front of Celerico, on the 20th; and Colonel Archibald Campbell's fine brigade the 6th and 18th regiments of Portuguese infantry, marched through this town on their route to the Val de Mondego.

On the following day Sir Brent Spencer, second in command, left this with his staff for Avelans de Riviera.

Regnier is reported to have arrived with his division at Zarza Mayor.

Yesterday and this morning it has rained violently, with thunder and lightning.

For the last 6 weeks the officers have amused themselves with frequent horse-races in this neighbourhood, and there was occasionally some good sport.

LETTER XXXV.

General Crawford retires over the Coa, after a smart affair with a greatly superior force of the Enemy.—General Hill's Division crosses the Tagus.—Regnier arrives at Castel Branco.—Movements of the British.—A party of Officers visit the Estrella.

Moimento de Sierra, 12*th August,* 1810.

On the 25th of July, at 3 A. M. the guards received orders to march; and soon after 6 proceeded through the small town of Baraçal to Marçal de Chao, 2 leagues, where they arrived about 8 o'clock. The cause of this sudden movement was owing to the enemy having passed the Coa in considerable force, after a severely contested affair with General R. Crawford's division.

During the whole of this day and the following, the wounded officers and men were passing to the rear in cars.

On the afternoon of the 26th, the enemy's advance appeared within a league of head-quarters, where preparations were made to receive them, the divisions of Generals Picton and Crawford being turned out for that purpose. The 14th and 16th dragoons take the duty of the out-posts.

Lieutenant-General Hill's division of the combined British and Portuguese army broke up from the left bank of the Tagus on the 17th ultimo, and crossing the river at Villa Velha, the head of the column reached Atalaya, 5 leagues on this side of Castel Branco, on the 22d.

Before day-break, on the 28th of July, the guards, left in front, with the brigade of guns attached to the division, moved out of the town of Marçal de Chao, and halted, to allow General Cameron's brigade to take its place in the column, which then retired through Baraçal, Celerico, Cortiço, and Villa Cortez, to Sampayo, where General Cameron's brigade was left; the guards proceeded about a league beyond to Gouvea, a handsome town, on the side of the Estrella. This day's march was one of the longest made by the British in Portugal, being upwards of 7 leagues. On the road passed the 4th dragoons, and Captain Bull's troop of horse artillery, going to the advance.

Next day the column was again in motion. About 8 A. M. the guards halted in Vinho; General Cameron's brigade marched a league further to Penhanços. At Vinho the arrival of the troops threw the inhabitants into the greatest consternation ; and a convent of nuns taking the alarm, the whole place became a scene of confusion. In the course of the day the friends of the poor Benedictines arrived from different parts of the country, and conveyed them away to a place of refuge, with the furniture of the nunnery. There was not a dry eye in the village as the affecting cavalcade set out; the poor had experienced the kindness of the nuns in a thousand instances, and lamented the hard necessity of their departure with unfeigned sorrow.

General Spencer remains at the out-posts, Fraxedas 2 leagues, in front of Alverca, with the light cavalry and horse artillery; head-quarters and General Crawford's light division are in Celerico, excepting only two companies of the 95th, stationed on the right bank of the Mondego.

General Picton's division is at Sampayo; General Cole's at Linhares, Mello, &c.; and the King's German legion at Gouvea.

Regnier has arrived at Castel Branco, with the 2d corps of the army, and Lieutenant-General Hill's division is watching his movements. Lieutenant-Colonel Wyndham of the royal dragoons was surprised and taken prisoner on a reconnoitreing party.

On the 3d instant the 3d guards marched to Moimento de Sierra, a beautiful village, 2 miles from Vinho, at the foot of the Estrella.

A party was formed to visit the highest point of the mountain, which is said to be 7000 feet above the level of the sea. The object of the officers was also to visit the lakes in that elevated situation.

The party set out from Moimento at an early hour, and passing through the small town of Cea, where the Bishop of Guarda has a palace, arrived about 9 o'clock at St. Romao, and procured a guide, who conducted them by a good road to a chapel close to the river Alva, 2 miles and a half from the last town. The road wound beautifully through a romantic country, under the rugged front of the Estrella, whence small streams were issuing in every direction, on their way to join the clear waters of the Alva. After this the road became a mere sheep-track, and so difficult that the party had to dismount and lead their mules. With much exertion they at last reached the furthest stage of the Estrella, where some rye was growing, and a few peasants thrashing. On enquiry they learned that the lakes were at the distance of 2 leagues. Every step the party advanced the scenery became more interesting, and the views more extensive; at one spot where a natural amphitheatre was formed, encircled by rocks, the sound was reverberated for a long period of time: here a large flock of goats were feeding. The road was now extremely intricate; at length the party reached the summit, and obtained a fine view of the Tralos Montes to the northward, and over an immense territory, bounded by the Atlantic in the west. The officers were several times enveloped in clouds, which at length dispersing, they left their mules and proceeded to the lakes; the greater forming nearly a square of 6 by 700 yards, was bounded on one side by a ridge of rocks, on which were some patches of snow; the lesser lake forms a kind of neck to the other. Some parts are so deep as never to have been fathomed; but this may be owing to the want of curiosity in the Portuguese. The party now returned, and at the end of 5 hours reached their mules.

There is some vegetation and a good deal of rye growing in the various Sierras. On the right, at the furthest extremity, is the ridge on which Guarda is situated. The few peasants whom the officers met with in this remote region of the air, informed them that wolves were numerous on different parts of the mountain; and here is to be found all the various genus of heath and plants: among others the dead plant is seen growing out of fissures in the rock, of a white colour, and appearing as if scorched by lightning.

The inhabitants of the villages situated in the Estrella have in their history the leading features of all mountain tribes; they pay no taxes, but one-tenth of the produce of their lands is assigned for the maintenance of a modern noble, and this tribute is collected half-yearly by his stewards.

The enemy, after establishing himself on the left bank of the Coa, commenced his preparations for the siege of Almeida, in which he proceeds but slowly, owing to the rocky soil, and the necessity of bringing earth from some distance, to cover his approaches. Marshal Ney a few days ago advanced with a considerable force for the purpose of making a *reconnoissance*, which having completed, he retired to his former position.

LETTER XXVI.

Almeida taken, and Retreat of the British.

Filhadoza, 31st of August, 1810.

AT day-break on the 19th instant, the guards were in motion, and advanced through the villages of Vinho, Sampayo, and Villa Cortez, to Linhares, a small town, with an ancient castle on the side of the Estrella; and the next day marched through Cortiço, to Celerico, 2 leagues.—Reports are favourable. Letters have been intercepted from some of the French generals, stating the misery and discontent of their troops, from sickness, want of pay, and the harassing warfare carried on by the Spaniards in every quarter.

On the 21st, head-quarters returned to Alverca da Beira; and on the 23d the guards again advanced to Marçal do Chao, and occupied their former cantonments.

Whether the exertions of the British will eventually secure the independence of these kingdoms or not, time alone can discover; meanwhile the position they have maintained for so many months, in the face of the most formidable French army on this side of the Pyrenees, has occasioned a diversion favourable to the Spaniards, by affording time to re-assemble and re-organize their troops, when defeated and dispersed by the superior military discipline and tactics of the enemy; and it forms a fine trait in their national character, that neither by threats or promises have any numbers been induced to abandon the cause of their country, and enrol themselves under the standard of the contemptible usurper.

The enemy having completed his works before Almeida, opened his batteries on the 26th instant, in the morning, and commenced a furious bombardment from 70 pieces of cannon, at the same moment. The besieged returned a very brisk fire during the whole of that day.

A telegraph was erected at head-quarters to communicate with Almeida; and it was said to be arranged, that the governor Colonel Cox, was to give notice to the Commander of the forces when he found a surrender unavoidable, on which the whole of the combined army in this quarter was to advance against the enemy, and driving him beyond the Coa, to bring off the garrison. The weather being hazy on the 27th, no message could be received by the telegraph, but it was perceived from the out-posts that the firing had ceased, and that the Governor was in communication with the enemy. In the absence of all information, various surmises were formed, and reports circulated, but the real cause of the disaster which compelled Colonel Cox to enter into terms with the enemy, remained for the present unknown.

August the 28th, a sudden order was issued at 10 A. M. when the guards marched to Celerico. Soon after leaving Marçal de Chao, a tremendous thunder-storm came on, accompanied with heavy rain. A private of the Coldstream was killed by a flash of lightning.—29th, to Gouvea, 4 leagues;—30th, to St. Romao, 2 leagues. The Coldstream halted in Cea.

This morning the 3d regiment arrived here, about half a mile from Saragoce, on the high road to Coimbra. The Coldstream in quarters at Torozello.—Distance from St. Romao, 1 league.

LETTER XXXVII.

The combined Army takes up a position on the right Bank of the Mondego.—Battle of Busaco.

St. Martinho do Bispo, 30th September, 1810.

On the morning of the 3d instant, the 1st division marched upon the road to Coimbra, 5 leagues. General Cameron's brigade and the 3d guards hutted; the Coldstream was quartered in Moita, and the King's German legion in an adjoining village.

Next day, the 3d guards marched to the village of Sanguinhada, and General Cameron's brigade on the 5th, was cantoned in Cortiço.

Head-quarters were at Gouvea, and every thing remained quiet in front. The 24th Portuguese regiment, taken in Almeida and said to have volunteered into the French service, has every man escaped.

At day-break on the 18th instant, the guards marched from Moita and Sanguinhada; at the same time, the rest of the division was in motion, and the whole crossed the Poute de Marcella and *bivouaced* 2 leagues beyond, near the village of Foy d'Arouce, on the banks of the river Ceira Thunder and lightning with heavy rains, which continued, without intermission, the whole of the night and following morning.

Before day-break on the 19th, the division was again on march, and entered Coimbra soon after mid-day.

Head-quarters were yesterday in Costiço, and this morning Lord Wellington with his staff, accompanied by Marshal Beresford, crossed the Mondego.

During the night, several Portuguese regiments came into Coimbra.

At half-past 9 A. M. on the 20th, the division advanced on the Oporto road and halted at Malheada, in which town, the 3d guards were quartered. The Coldstream halted in a wood on the right. Colonel Packenham's brigade, the 7th and 79th were in advance, Lord Blantyre (Cameron's) on the left, and the King's German legion half a mile in the rear.

September the 21st, before dawn, the division was under arms. The 3d guards moved out of Malheada to join the Coldstream, when Colonel Packenham's brigade went into cantonments. Several brigades of Portuguese infantry formed in the rear of the division on the Coimbra road.

September the 22d the Coldstream went into quarters at Valcaliza, the 3d regiment in the villages of Travossa and Canedo.

The fall of Almeida after a bombardment of only one day, but in reality, occasioned by the explosion of the grand magazine; by which unfortunate event, one half of the town was destroyed, 500 of the garrison, and a great number of the inhabitants killed, removed the principal remaining obstacle to the entrance of Massena's army into this kingdom, but they proceeded with great caution in their movements, owing to the difficulty of bringing forward their supplies, which was absolutely necessary, as the enemy could not place any dependence on the resources of a country so long occupied by the British. The French appear to have been completely foiled in their plans, by the prudent defensive system adopted by Lord Wellington, as there can be no doubt that it was a principal object with Massena, in undertaking the sieges of Ciudad Rodrigo and Almeida, to draw the British from their strong hilly positions to the plains on which these towns are situated; where, if at all, the superior number of his cavalry might be expected to give him the advantage. On a further advance from the frontier, that species of force could no longer be rendered useful in the same degree, but must prove extremely burdensome and embarrassing to his operations, from the very great scarcity of forage, which even the British experienced at times, although the harvest had been got in, and the whole grain in the country was in requisition for their supply.

About a fortnight ago, Marshal Massena made a feint of coming down upon the left bank of the Mondego, and actually pushed his reconnoitreing parties to Cortiço and Linhares in that direction, but, apprehensive of meeting a check at the strong pass of the

Ponte de Marcella, he, on the 18th, 19th, and 20th of September crossed the river with his whole army at the bridge of Fornos, below Celerico, advancing upon Coimbra by the way of Vizeu. This movement of the enemy was met by the Commander of the forces with his usual foresight, and the intentions of the French leader being now clearly developed, the 2d division under General Hill was directed to join the main body by the route of Sobriera Formosa and Pedro-gao, when the whole of the combined army, with the exception of General Fane's division of cavalry and some Portuguese infantry, was placed upon the right bank of the Mondego, with a celerity which set all ordinary calculation at defiance.

September the 22d, skirmishing at the out-posts.

On the 23d, the bridge over the Criz beyond Mortigao having been blown up by Brigadier-General Pack, the French occupied themselves in repairing it, and then passed over a column of infantry and cavalry, who were opposed by the light division and General Pack's Portuguese brigade.

On the 24th and 25th the enemy continued to advance, and it was evident the whole of his force was concentrating. In a smart skirmish, Captain Hoey was severely and Mellish slightly wounded.

Whilst the French continued their approach upon Coimbra by the road leading over the Sierra of Busaco, the main body of the allied army remained in the adjoining villages, where the troops had been cantoned, that they might not suffer from the heavy dews at this season of the year.

Before day-break on the 26th the several divisions of British and Portuguese were in motion. The brigade of guards arrived in the village of Luz about 8 o'clock, and soon after began to ascend the Sierra of Busaco, on whose summit is situated, a convent of the austere order of La Trappe, Lord Wellington's head-quarters. The route lay for nearly 2 miles through the gardens; before leaving them, a cannonade commenced, the brigade was ordered to load and then formed behind the brow of the hill, from whence, the whole of the enemy's force was distinctly discerned. They appeared in considerable numbers, the infantry supposed to be not less than 60,000, and a very large force in cavalry.

About 5 P. M. the French piquets made an attack upon the Portuguese light troops, (casadores,) who returned their fire with the utmost steadiness and resolution.

The formation of the combined army was as follows:—

Lieutenant-General Hill's division, which had crossed the Mondego this morning, was placed on the right of the whole line, having the divisions of Generals Leith and Picton on his left. In the centre, the 1st division, of which the guards formed the right, under the command of Sir Brent Spencer, beyond was the light division in the most advanced part of the position, opposite the gardens of the monastery. Major-General Cole's at the extremity on the left.

General Fane's division of cavalry remained on the left bank of the Mondego, to observe the movements of the enemy in that direction: a few squadrons only were on the heights, the ground being unfavourable for that description of force; and the main body under Sir Stapleton Cotton was formed in the plains in front of Malheada, and on the Oporto road.

The brigades of Portuguese infantry and casadores were united with the British, and the result proved this to have been the best possible distribution of the troops of our ally.

The line of the combined army thus posted, extended along the ridge of Busaco for nearly 2 leagues, but the whole of the intermediate space was not occupied, except by a chain of light troops, and formed the segment of a circle, whose extreme points embraced every part of the enemy's position. Not a movement could be made in the French lines without its being immediately observed from the Sierra, and this circumstance contributed most materially to the success of the British.

At dusk, the 1st division moved to the right, and *bivouaced* close to the brow of the hill covered by the light infantry. The weather thick and foggy.

September the 27th at dawn of day the enemy advanced 2 columns, and at the same moment, threatened the right and centre of the allied army. The column on the right moved up the hill, under the fire of the light troops, with great intrepidity, and had gained the summit, when it was charged whilst deploying into line, in the most gallant manner by Colonel Mackinnon's brigade, the 45th and 88th regiments, and the 9th Portuguese under Lieutenant-Colonel Sutton, supported on the right by part of General Leith's corps, and on the left by Major-General Lightburne's brigade and the guards, which had moved to the right for that purpose, on the first indication of the enemy's intention. The French could not withstand the shock, but retreated down the hill with immense loss. One regiment, the 1st *Legere* of Regnier's *Corps d'Armee* was entirely cut to pieces. The enemy foiled in this attack, made another more to the right, where he was again repulsed at the point of the bayonet. This second attack was supported by some heavy artillery, and dismounted 2 guns; but a shell having set fire to the ammunition tumbril which blew up, the French abandoned their battery.

The Commander of the forces was every where in person, giving directions and superintending the different points of attack. Early in the morning, two of his staff, Lieutenant-Colonel Campbell and Lord Fitzroy Somerset were wounded.

Finding these attacks on the right unsuccessful, the enemy directed his principal efforts against the left of the centre, and in a charge made by the 43d and 52d regiments, General Simon was wounded and taken with his Aid-de-Camp. A short time afterwards a young Spanish lady, in male attire, whom the General had carried off from Madrid, and his baggage, were sent to the British head-quarters with a flag of truce.

About 8 o'clock a fog came on, which, for a time, partially obscured the positions of the respective armies. When the day cleared up, it was discovered that the enemy had placed large bodies of light troops in the woods and valley which skirted the bottom of the Sierra. They were successfully opposed by the light division, the casadores, the light infantry of the 1st division, and

Colonel Pakenham's brigade the 7th, and 79th regiments. The enemy's fire slackened about noon, but the light troops continued engaged until the evening. During the action, a number of deserters came over.

On the following morning the light infantry were again partially engaged on the left of the line. At mid-day the enemy's cavalry and several columns of infantry were observed in motion to the rear. All quiet in camp. The French set fire to a small village on leaving it.

At 10 P. M. the army quitted the position of Busaco. After halting for 2 hours near the monastery, the 1st division proceeded on the road to Coimbra. At day-light on the 29th, it was perceived that the enemy had withdrawn the whole of his troops from the ground he occupied during the engagement.

An hour before sun-set the division halted within a league of Coimbra, and this morning the troops were again under arms before daybreak. About 8 o'clock the guards in the rear of the column forded the Mondego, and went into quarters in the village of St

Martinho do Bispo. Strong picquets were formed to protect the fords during the night.

A detachment of the guards joined this day from England, having come round by sea from Lisbon to Figueiras.

LETTER XXXVIII.

The Combined Army retires to the entrenched Position, in the vicinity of Lisbon, &c.

Portella de Casaes, 10th November, 1810.

THE manœuvres of Marshal Massena, after the battle of Busaco, left the Commander of the forces, in no doubt of his intention to throw his whole army on the high road, from Oporto, and the position being turned on the 29th of September, by the enemy's movement to the right, Lord Wellington, in pursuance of the defensive system, on which he had hitherto acted, commenced his retreat to the fortified lines in the neighbourhood of the capital.

On the 1st of October, Sir Brent Spencer's division moved out of their cantonments before day-break, and passing through the town of Periera and Souré *bivouaced* at dusk, in a vineyard close to the latter. The roads were crouded with people flying from their houses to the mountains and sea coast, the monasteries and nunneries were deserted numbers accompanied the march of the British troops, and the banks of the Mondego were lined with distressed groupes, impatiently waiting to embark.

The advance of the enemy on this morning entered Coimbra, their cavalry having previously charged a troop of horse artillery, which retired without loss over the Mondego.

October the 2nd, After a fatiguing march of 5 leagues, on a road parallel with the one through Pombal, by which the main body of the army was retiring, the 1st division halted on the banks of the Rio Maganche, within a league of Leyria, through which the troops marched next morning, and *bivouaced* in a wood, a league and a half beyond, near Canvieza, until the 5th, when the columns were again in motion, and halted at the close of day, near the village of Condieras.

On the 6th, through Riomayor to Alcoentre, 4 leagues, and on the 7th, to Aldea Gallega, the same distance. The army each day in *bivouac*.

Heavy rains set in on the following morning, and the roads were in a dreadful state.

The 1st division passed through Sobral, about noon, and the battalions were cantoned in the adjoining villages. The guards at San Quintino, within a short distance of the works.

The cavalry under Sir Stapleton Cotton, covered the retreat of the army, during the whole of the march from Busaco, and on several occasions, particularly at Leyria, on the 5th instant proved its decided superiority over that of the enemy.

October the 9th, heavy rains. The troops remained in their quarters. The state of the roads necessarily retarded the enemy's advance to the position.

October the 10th, the whole division in Sobral. The commander of the forces, and Marshal Beresford, arrived at San Quintino. Next day the troops marched from Sobral, at 2 in the afternoon, and remained until dusk, on the brow of a hill, in front of the grand batteries. Afterwards the guards moved into the village of Sobriera. Heavy rains, with thunder and lightning, but the enemy continued to advance, notwithstanding the severity of the weather.

October the 12th, all quiet. The troops were kept in readiness to turn out at a moment's notice.

On the 13th, a strong column of the enemy was observed on the height, beyond Sobral, apparently moving towards the left. The gun boats, under the command of Lieutenant Berkeley, stationed in the Tagus, abreast of Villa Franca, opened a heavy fire this morning upon the town, in which there was a French force of 1200 men, who were driven out, with considerable loss. General Lacroix was cut in two by a cannon shot.

Working parties were employed in completing the works on Sobriera Hill, and in mending the road to Bucellas. The high road to Mafra runs through this village. All quiet during the night.

About noon on the 14th, the enemy opened a battery of four-pounders, from behind some casks, at the entrance of Sobral, upon the advance of the 1st division, consisting of the 71st regiment, under Colonel Cadogan, and part of Major-General Cameron's brigade. After a severe conflict of an hour, the enemy's fire was discontinued, and each party carried off their wounded. In this affair the French lost 100 men, British, 40, in killed and wounded. A few prisoners were taken, but no advantage gained on either side. The picquets remained at dusk within a short distance of Sobral, which was occupied by the enemy, whose force being increased towards the evening, by the arrival of the 8th corps, and part of the 6th, Sir Brent Spencer, in the course of the night, withdrew his advanced posts.

At day-break the next morning, a reconnoitreing party of the enemy was observed on the heights, where Major-General Cameron's brigade was posted the day before. About 7 A. M. the light infantry of the guards, moved out of Cabedos, in which a company of the 60th was left. Several working parties employed in mining the roads for explosion. The report of Colonel Trant, having taken 5000 of the enemy's sick and wounded, in Coimbra, has reached the French army, and creatse a considerable sensation among the troops, whom the officers are endeavouring to persuade that the news is unfounded.

Massena attended by a large staff, was distinctly seen reconnoitreing yesterday, for a considerable time. His army is in 3 divisions, and the right does not appear to be advanced beyond Sobral, his left, extended to the Tagus. The road to Torres Vedras, is rendered nearly impassable, by the rains, which still continue, although not so violent as during the last week. It is generally believed that the French are in a very awkward predicament, in consequence of their rapid advance. Massena has met with an opposition he certainly did not expect, and his difficulties are hourly increasing, from the want of provisions.

At 5 P. M. the guards moved out of Sobriera to Portella de Casaes, to make room for Major-General Sir W. Erskine's brigade.

The following is the disposition of the combined army:—

2d division—
 Hill's, the right resting at Alhandra. on the Tagus, and flanked by gun-

boats. The brigades of Generals Lumley and Hoghton, at Bucellas.

Light division, Crawford's,
5th ditto, Leith's } under canvas.

1st division—
    Sir B. Spencer, centre and left. The General's head-quarters in Sobriera.

3d division—
    Picton's, Torres Vedras.

4th division—
    Cole's, Dias Portas.

6th division—
    A. Campbell's, Ribaldiera.

Cavalry.—Head-quarters of Sir S. Cotton, at Mafra.

The Portuguese brigades in the batteries, and intermixed with the British Brigadeir-General Pack commands in the fort, on the most elevated point, and in the centre of the intrenched line. From this spot, which is immediately above the village of Portella de Casaes, there is a most beautiful and extensive view; comprehending on the right, the rich valley of the Tagus, and across that river into the province of Alentejo, and on the left, to the Atlantic, including the whole of the positions, the hill of Cintra, and the Burlings—with the fortress of Peniche.

October 16th, all quiet—the sick sent daily to Lisbon. Working parties employed on the works, and in repairing some roads, and blocking up others. Communications to the Commander of the forces, sent by the telegraphs on the hills, under the command of naval officers, and signals for the several brigades to march to their respective alarm posts, directed to be made on the first appearance of a forward movement by the enemy.

On the 19th, the Marquis of Romana, crossed the Tagus below Villa Franca, with the 1st division of the Spanish army, under General O'Donnell.

The principal part of the French infantry have hutted in a pine wood, about a league in rear of Sobral, which they continue to occupy. The enemy has no troops to the right of that town, therefore it is supposed that the attack when made with a view of penetrating to Lisbon, will be either by the high road, leading from Sobral, to that city, or by the road on the bank of the Tagus, which in addition to the troops and batteries in that part of the line is flanked by the gunboats, under Lieutenant Berkeley, who has already driven him out of Villa Franca. Massena seems at no time to have entertained the idea of forcing his way to the capital, by the road on the sea side, from Torres Vedras, through Mafra and Cintra.

October the 28th, the heavy rains have been succeeded for the last week, by fine dry healthy weather, the mornings cold. Deserters continue to arrive, who affirm that the enemy's baggage is sent to the rear, and that a considerable force, under Loison, has already fallen back upon Thomar, doubtless with a view of collecting provisions, of which particularly bread, the troops are in great want. The accounts of deserters, however, are always to be received with extreme jealousy and caution.

Brigadier-General Blunt has sent out parties from Peniché, who are constantly harassing the enemys right; several skirmishes have taken place near Obidos, where there is a small Portuguese garrison commanded by Captain Fenwick.

Major-General Fane, has crossed the Tagus, with a division of cavalry and infantry to prevent the enemy foraging in the Alentejo.

The enemy's force on his left seems to have rather increased. Massena was observed making a *reconnoissance* yesterday.

November the 7th, Marshal Beresford was invested with the Insignia of the Bath in the royal palace of Mafra, on which occasion the Commander of the British forces gave a splendid entertainment to the officers of the army and to the Portuguese nobility.

The enemy remains in *statu quo*, and nothing of importance has lately taken place.

LETTER XXXIX.

Retreat of the French.—The British in pursuit, arrive before Santarem, where General R. Crawford is left to watch the Enemy, &c.

Cartaxo, November 25, 1810.

AT day-light, on the 15th instant, it was perceived that the enemy's piquets were withdrawn, and soon afterwards that he had quitted Sobral, and was in full retreat on the road to Santarem. At midnight the troops received orders to march. At daybreak the brigade of guards moved off, passing through Sobral, and at 2 P. M. arrived in Alemquer, where Massena's head-quarters had been for some time.—The day remarkably foggy.—The French had placed fire beacons on every height.—Alemquer is beautifully situated in a valley, watered by a small river. Here is a very large paper manufactory, the only one in the kingdom.

The whole place exhibited the usual marks of its having been possessed by the enemy, every house being left in a most dirty state. Nothing escaped the unpitying hand of the French; the furniture in many houses was destroyed, although it appeared that they had gone off without much previous notice. The churches were not spared by the enemy; on the contrary, every thing appertaining to religion seemed marked for particular destruction. The deserted nunnery was completely ransacked.

November the 17th, the 1st division halted in Alemquer, where head-quarters also remained. Next morning the troops were under arms before day-break, and passing through Carregada, Villa Nova, and Azambujo, arrived about 4 P. M. in the town of Cartaxo, which the enemy had pillaged. Lieutenant-General Hill crossed the Tagus, at Valada, on his route towards Abrantes.

Previous to the march it was said that the enemy's rear guard had evacuated Santarem; but this information proving incorrect, the Commander of the forces reconnoitred the position which the French had taken up, and determined to attack them on the following morning.

November the 19th, the division, left in front, marched from Cartaxo at day-break, and at 8 o'clock halted on a plain to allow the rear of the column to close up; after which the troops proceeded on the road to Santarem, which they arrived in sight of about 9 o'clock. General Anson's brigade of cavalry was detached on the Riomayor road; several corps of British and Portuguese infantry were also moving upon the enemy's right.

The plan of attack had been already communicated to the general officers. The light division was to advance along the marshy plain which extends to the Tagus on the right; Sir William Erskine's brigade was to engage the enemy's attention on the left; whilst the brigade of guards, preceded by the light companies, and supported by Major-General Cameron's Highland brigade, pushed across the bridge and narrow causeway to storm the lower range of heights, on which the French were discovered in considerable force. This part of the attack must inevitably have been attended with loss; the bridge over the Riomayor and causeway being completely commanded by the enemy's artillery, abbattis constructed, and other impediments thrown in the way of the British. Every exertion had been made to render the position tenable, and certainly the whole presented a most formidable aspect. Besides these apparent obstacles to an attack, it was supposed that the causeway was mined for explosion.—Admitting, however, that these difficulties had been overcome by the valour and perseverance of the troops, it is doubtful whether the British could have maintained their ground on the lower ridge, exposed to a heavy cannonade from Santarem and the adjoining range of heights, to which the ascent was extremely difficult of approach, the road leading over another causeway similarly commanded as the first by the guns of the enemy. During the whole of this day, the Commander of the forces continued his *reconnoissance*, and in the evening the troops went into quarters, the guards in the village of Vallé, leaving strong piquets to secure the front; the advanced sentry was posted on the bridge, about 150 yards from those of the French, whose piquet was stationed on the opposite bank.

Before day-break on the 20th, the brigades assembled at their respective alarm-posts, and remained under arms until dusk. At 11 A. M. the light division and a squadron of the royal dragoons advanced along the low marshy plain towards the enemy's left, and commenced firing on his out-posts; but the ground was so unfavourable that Brigadier-General Crawford soon retired, in which movement he was not molested by the enemy.—The rain of the preceding night had completely inundated the plain, and swelled the river, over which a bridge of trees was thrown, about half a mile below the one communicating with the causeway.

Head-quarters in Cartaxo, where General Leith's division and the King's German legion are also cantoned.

General Hill's division was observed this morning on march, on the south bank of the Tagus.

November the 22d, about 2 P. M. the troops were ordered under arms, and the baggage sent off to the rear of Cartaxo, in consequence of the enemy making a movement on the left. General Pack's brigade of

Portuguese infantry, which had advanced towards his right, was obliged to retire after some skirmishing, the whole of the 8th corps, Junot's, being drawn out for the purpose of making a *reconnoissance*, which having completed, the French returned to Santarem. The 2d *corps d' armee* is also said to be in that town ; and Marshal Ney with the 6th, betwixt Thomar and the Zezere.

On the 23d Sir Brent Spencer withdrew the guards and General Cameron's brigade into Cartaxo, where head-quarters remain. The light division continues advanced in front, supported by a brigade of cavalry, observing the enemy ; General Picton's division is at Torres Vedras ; General A. Campbell's at Alemquer ; General Cole's at Azambujo ; and General Leith's upon the left at Alcoentre, &c. The 2d division Lieutenant-General Hill's, and Major-General Fane's division of cavalry remain on the left bank of the Tagus. Sir William Erskine commands the advance.

It was for a day or two supposed that Massena intended to withdraw his army from Portugal ; but it would now appear this was never in his contemplation, his sole object being to place his troops in good winter quarters, until the arrival of the expected reinforcements from France, which " Son Altesse d'Essling" has been enabled to accomplish, by the possession of Santarem, the strongest place on either bank of the Tagus.

Massena was easily enabled to mask his movement to the rear, as his troops were constantly in motion on the road betwixt the position and Santarem. Having gradually withdrawn the main body, his piquets were called in without any previous notice, after dusk on the 14th; and as no deserters came over on that night, his retreat was not discovered until day-light next morning. The light division immediately advanced in pursuit, but some delay took place in respect to the cavalry, who were never enabled to bring the enemy's rear guard to action; consequently few prisoners were made.

LETTER XL.

The French after retiring from before the fortified position in the vicinity of the Capital, are cantoned during the Winter Months in Santarem, Thomar, &c.—Death of the Marquis of Romana.—Sketch of his Character, &c.

Cartaxo, 20th February, 1811.

THE enemy continues to maintain himself in the strong position of Santarem, and the three corps of the army under the immediate command of Massena, are cantoned in Thomar, Torres Novas, and the other towns and villages in the fertile district betwixt Santarem and the Zezere, over which river he has thrown a bridge, and collected a number of boats with the intention, it is supposed, of transporting his army across the Tagus, into the province of Alentejo. He has also constructed a battery on the rising ground, above the town of Punhete, and his guns command the navigation of both rivers. Notwithstanding these advantages, however, the combined force under Marshal Sir W. C. Beresford, judiciously posted on the left bank of the Tagus, is considered sufficiently formidable to oppose the passage of the enemy with every probability of success.

The French troops have hitherto drawn the whole of their supplies from this district, and it is known that the resources of the country are in consequence nearly exhausted. The enemy's excursions in quest of provisions and forage for his cavalry are always made to the rear, and extremely confined, owing to the vigilance of the ordenenza, who lose no opportunity of cutting off stragglers, and continually carry on a most harassing and destructive warfare.

General Gardanne's division which had arrived within a short distance of the Zezere, about the end of November, became alarmed on the appearance of a small reconnoitreing party from the garrison of Abrantes, which made some prisoners, and retired in great confusion towards the frontier, followed by the ordenenza, who annoyed them considerably during their retreat, and captured a quantity of baggage. This division subsequently formed a junction with the 9th corps, commanded by General Drouet, two divisions of which taking the route of the Ponte de Marcella, arrived at Leyria in December, where this General has established his head-quarters; having opened his communication with the main body of the invading army, by a chain of posts extending across the country to Pernis, where the enemy has thrown up some field works. General Claparede occupies Guarda, with another division, having his advance in Belmonte; and the remaining battalions of the 9th corps form the garrisons of Almeida, Ciudad Rodrigo, and Salamanca.

Colonel Downie, who arrived from England with dispatches on the 9th of December, proceeded afterwards to Badajos, having received permission from the Spanish government to raise a legion of 3000 men in the province of Estremadura.

An Aid-de-Camp of Massena's has been taken prisoner, disguised as a peasant. On his person was found a letter addressed to the first French General commanding a division with whom he could meet. Aware that the circumstances under which he was taken will affect his life, agreeably to the usages of war, it is not improbable but that thus situated, he may have given Lord Wellington some information of importance, which of course is not suffered to transpire.

Deserters are continually coming in, who report that the enemy is destitute of bread, and the troops have neither wine nor spirits. These articles are absolutely requisite, and essential to the health of the army, at such a season of the year, and in a climate like this. The statement of deserters however, must always be received with some degree of distrust; but the present accounts are corroborated by the inhabitants of Thomar and Torres Novas, who had generally remained in their habitations on the arrival of the French, and have now quitted them in a starving condition.

The enemy moved a considerable force of infantry and cavalry towards the left, and drove the British piquets through the town of Rio Mayor on the 19th ulti o. Whatever was their object on this occasion, they soon after retired. General Junot, who commanded the troops, was wounded in the face by a ball from a rifle.

Don Julien Sanchez, whose activity is unremitting, has had the address to capture a large convoy of biscuit, which was destined for the army of Portugal near Ciudad Rodrigo.

The engineers have latterly been employed in throwing up works betwixt Trafraria and Almada, on the south bank of the Tagus; and a canal has also been cut across the neck of land to Setuval.—These operations will completely insure the safety of the numerous shipping in the river.

On the 23d of January the cause of the peninsula sustained an irreparable loss in the lamented death of the Marquis de la Romana. He had been indisposed for some days previously with spasms in his chest, but finding himself much better on that morning, he dressed, with the intention of paying a visit to Lord Wellington, when a sudden return of his complaint rendered it necessary to send for medical assistance, which proved unavailing, the attack being of so violent a nature as to terminate in the short space of half an hour, his valuable existence.

The death of such a man at any time, must have been considered as a national calamity; at the present moment it is matter of deep regret, that his country should have been deprived of a character, from his talents and patriotism, so truly estimable.

The Marquis was educated in France, and spoke the language with the fluency of a native; he had resided there at different periods, and formed many friendships, but all personal considerations gave place to the sacred love of his country, which with him was an innate principle that glowed in his bosom, and formed a distinguished feature in his noble character. It was this *Amor patriæ* that taught him constantly to deprecate the ascendancy which France so long maintained over the feeble councils of the Spanish monarchy.

Buonaparte must be supposed to have possessed some knowledge of Romana's sentiments being inimical to his views, and consequently dreading the influence of his example upon the conduct and minds of his countrymen, he practised that *finesse*, which, for a time, removed the Marquis and his brave associates far from their native land. In this isolated situation, neither his patriotism nor his firmness for a moment forsook him; the resources of his mind became gradually unfolded, as occasions called them forth, and his unceasing efforts, aided by Great Britain, at length restored him and his companions to the service of their country. From the period of his return, the Marquis continually exerted himself in the cabinet and in the field, to frustrate the designs of the usurper. No motives of private ambition governed his actions; the independence of Spain was the sole object of his cares, and most truly, most justly was his zealous conduct and unshaken loyalty appreciated by a grateful and admiring people.

At all times affable and easy of access, the Marquis of Romana possessed the mild conciliating manners of a perfect gentleman. With the courtesy peculiar to his disposition, he listened to every one, and his excellent judgment, unfettered by prejudice, enabled him to estimate and decide with promptitude, on those measures which were submitted to his consideration. The mind of this illustrious patriot was, indeed, most clear and comprehensive; and it is certain, that he possessed more talents for business than the management of an army, to which, his genius was not so well suited; although, at an early period of life, he had adopted the military profession and attained considerable rank.

The remains of the noble Marquis were conveyed to Vallada on the morning of the 26th, with suitable honours.

The procession led by the grenadiers of Major-General Nightingall's brigade, with arms reversed, moved at a slow pace through the town of Cartaxo; the band of the 79th regiment playing the mournful, yet beautiful and appropriate air " To the land of the Leal."

Next followed a squadron of cavalry, and a few paces in their rear came the body in a car drawn by 6 horses. On the coffin, which was covered with crimson velvet, were placed the hat and sword of the late Marquis.

At a short distance from the car Lord Wellington and Sir Brent Spencer with their Aides-de-Camp, and a number of Officers attended to pay the last tribute of respect to the illustrious deceased.

On their arrival at Vallada, the body was put into a barge commanded by a Lieutenant of the navy and conveyed to Lisbon, where a vault was prepared for its reception, until an opportunity shall offer of removing it to Majorca, in which island, the principal estates of the Marquis are situated; and his family, consisting of the Marchioness, a son, and daughter, at present reside.

LETTER XLI.

Retreat of Massena from Santarem, and advance of the British.—Operations during the Pursuit, which is continued until the whole of the Army of Portugal cross the Agueda, leaving Almeida to its fate.—French barbarity.

Almadilla, Spain, 15th April, 1811.

INTELLIGENCE having reached the British head-quarters in the beginning of March, that the enemy had been for some days employed in sending his heavy artillery and baggage, with the sick, to the rear, it became evident that the French Commander in Chief had some important movement in contemplation. On the 4th a large convent in Santarem was perceived on fire; at dusk on the following days the enemy withdrew his picquets, and the whole of the remaining force evacuated the town about midnight.

On the morning of the 5th of March, General Picton's division moved forward, the enemy having withdrawn his troops from the vicinity of Rio Mayor.

Soon after day-break on the 6th the light division entered Santarem, and, in the course of that day, the 1st, 4th, and 6th divisions of infantry arrived in the town. The enemy during his stay, had omitted no means of improving his position, which, in consequence, was found remarkably strong. It appears that there were never more than 5 or 6 regiments in Santarem, and those very sickly, which agrees with the accounts uniformly received from prisoners and deserters.

The light division arrived about noon at Pernis, which the rear-guard of the French quitted before day-light, having effectually destroyed the 2 arches of the bridge. These, however, were spedily repaired by the staff corps for the passage of infantry.

On the 7th the troops were under arms at an early hour, when the guards and King's German legion marched to Pernis, the 4th and 6th divisions to Golegao. Head-quarters on this day, at Torres Novas.

Pernis, where Junot had been stationed for some weeks, is situated in a fertile valley, watered by the Aveila in its course to the Tagus. About 200 yards above the bridge, the river, tumbling over broken rocks, forms a grand and romantic cascade, the banks being extremely confined and fringed with wood, through which the stream is seen rushing, add to the beauty of the surrounding objects, A ruined mill, covered with ivy, and some old houses overhanging the river, contiguous to the fall, contribute further to enrich the scenery, which is in the highest degree picturesque. Under a projection of the cliff lay the mutilated remains of a Frenchman, who, having straggled from his party, had been put to death by the peasantry.

There were few inhabitants in Pernis, and those in great distress for want of subsistence, the French having on their arrival, seized on every article of provision for their own use, regardless of the misery this occasioned to the wretched Portuguese.

On the 8th the artillery of the 1st division crossed the river at the ford a little below the bridge, and were parked on the opposite heights; the troops remained in their quarters, ready to move at a moment's notice.

March the 9th, the main body of the French under Massena have taken the Coimbra road. General Regnier, with the 2d corps, is marching towards Espinhel, and Loison's division by Anciao.

About 10 o'clock the guards and King's German legion marched from Pernis, and at 3 P. M. reached Torres Novas, for some time Massena's head-quarters. At 5 the brigade was again in motion, and in 4 hours the 3d regiment halted in the village of Sudes, where there were few inhabitants. Roads very bad. The guns in consequence took a circuitous route to the right through Atalaya.

On the 10th the 3d regiment advanced to Pyalvo, where the Coldstream had been cantoned the preceding night. The brigade then proceeded on march, and about noon came up with the rear of the 4th division on the road from Thomar to Leyria. General Cole had been ordered across the Tagus to reinforce Marshal Beresford, but was recalled, on Massena's movement being distinctly ascertained. In the afternoon heavy showers of rain. About 4 P. M. halted near the miserable village of Caçhairas. Colonel De Grey's brigade of cavalry, the King's German legion, and 4th division on the same ground. The whole of the troops in *bivouac*. Before dusk Major-General Hoghton's corps from the 2d division reached the camp.

At day-break on the 11th of March, the troops were in motion, and proceeded left in front on the road to Pombal; the 6th division joined the column, the head of which, after a long and fatiguing march, arrived near the town at dusk. Pombal had been set on fire by the enemy, who failed in his attempt to hold the ancient castle, and was driven out by the light division. About 9 P. M. the enemy's fires in front of the town were observed going out; but a considerable force remained in *bivouac*, at the distance of a league.

The whole of the army was collected near Pombal in the course of this evening.

Next morning, (the 12th) the British columns advanced along the road to Condeixa, part of the troops fording the river, while the rest moved over the bridge and through the town, in pursuit of the enemy, whose rear guard, commanded this day by Marshal Ney, was brought to action in front of the village of Redinha, their right on the Souré river screened by a wood; from whence, after a gallant stand, they were dislodged by Sir Brent Spencer, with the 3d, 4th, and light divisions, and the troops following the enemy briskly across the narrow bridge over the Redinha river drove him upon the main body at Condeixa. During this operation, the remaining divisions were in reserve. The army *bivouaced* for the night close to Redinha. The 6th division under General A. Campbell made a lateral movement this morning upon the enemy's right by way of Souré.

On the 13th the allied army was again in motion at day-break. The main body with the artillery marched upon the high road, while General Picton advanced along the heights on the right, with some mountain guns. Soon after mid-day the columns closed up and *bivouaced* within a league of Condeixa, which was observed on fire. The light division was, for a short time, partially engaged with the enemy's rear.

March the 14th the troops moved off their ground about 7 o'clock, and advanced towards Condeixa. In several places the enemy had constructed abattis to retard the pursuit: these obstacles, however, were soon overcome, and the columns, with the exception of Major-General Picton's division which moved along the heights and manœuvred upon the enemy's left, passed through the once beautiful, but now ruined town of Condeixa. Meanwhile, the light division, supported by the 6th, was warmly engaged with the enemy, whose sharp-shooters, advantageously posted behind stone walls, took a deliberate aim upon the advance of the British. This irregular warfare continued for some hours; after which, the enemy retired to a hill, 1 league in front of Miranda de Corvo, in consequence of the movements made on his flanks by General Picton and the light division under Sir William Erskine. From a height on which the light division *bivouaced*, the French were observed in considerable force. Regnier, who had taken the Espinhel road, followed by Major-General Nightingall, effected à junction this day with the main body under the Prince of Esling, whose whole army was now assembled in one solid mass.

In the course of the morning several Officers were wounded. Major Stewart of the 95th, Captain Napier of the 43d, and Captain George T. Napier of the 52d. Major Napier of the 50th who had been severely wounded in the battle of Corunna, was sent for to his brothers, when a most affecting scene took place.

March the 15th.—The morning was extremely foggy, which proved favourable to the enemy, whose movements were thereby concealed. About 9 the day cleared up, previous to which, the light division under Sir William Erskine, 3d, (Picton's) and 6th, (A. Campbell's) advanced in pursuit. Some deserters came in, who said that the French were destroying their artillery and burning a quantity of ammunition. At 11, the 1st division marched, and about 3 P. M. passed through the smoking ruins of Miranda de Corvo. The roads throughout were strewed with animals, destroyed carriages and baggage, and numbers of dead and wounded

Frenchmen. At 5, the light division and Major-General Picton's, supported by the 1st and 6th divisions and 2 brigades of cavalry, brought the enemy's rear to action near the village of Foy d'Arouce. The firing continued until dusk, when the French retreated in confusion and with considerable loss across the Ceira river, in which many were drowned.

On the 16th of March at 4 A. M. the enemy blew up the bridge over the Ceira, keeping a force on the opposite bank to watch the fords. This day the army halted for supplies, which there was found some difficulty in bringing forward; the roads at all times bad, having been much cut up by the late heavy rains. General Cole and Colonel de Grey have proceeded to join Marshal Beresford in the Alentejo.

On the 17th of March the enemy's rear guard moved off during the night, and at day-break the advance of the British forded the river near the bridge. Soon after the 1st division crossed at a ford, about a mile above, upon which the enemy had brought two guns to bear on the preceding day.

On the 18th of March the army advanced towards the Ponte de Marcella, over which the whole of the enemy had now retired and destroyed the bridge, leaving a strong corps to observe the ford. About 2 P. M. the 1st division halted near the village of Pombeiro, where Lord Wellington fixed his head-quarters. The enemy was posted in force, on the right bank of the Alva. During the whole of this retreat, the French made their marches by night, putting their troops in motion a few hours after dusk.

The 19th of March.—This morning thick and foggy; in consequence, the troops remained in their huts until noon, when the fog dispersed. The 3d division marched to Arganil; about 5, the guards at the head of the 1st division arrived on the bank of the Alva, which they forded mid-deep: night coming on, the 5th division halted on the left bank. There was some difficulty in getting the artillery across.

A number of prisoners were made on this day, having been sent out for the purpose of collecting provisions in the neighbouring villages; and from this circumstance, it is believed to have been Massena's intention to have halted on the right bank of the Alva to refresh his army, had he not found himself so closely pursued. The troops *bivouaced* in the position of Moita, where they remained waiting for their supplies until noon on the 25th, when the column proceeded on the road to Celerico. At dusk the 1st division halted near the village of Galizes. The 5th division, Major-General Dunlop's, in the rear, within a short distance.

At day-break on the 26th, the British advanced 4 leagues, and about dusk the guards went into quarters at St. Martinho and St. Marinha; Major-General Howard's at St. Romao; General Nightingall's at Cea, and the King's German legion at Penhanços. Artillery at the Quinta de Beca, which, with the palace at Cea, had been burnt to the ground. Head-quarters in Gouvea, 3d division, General Picton's, at Linhares. The advance at Celerico, in which the enemy have destroyed a few houses.

On the 27th, halted.

On the 28th the division advanced towards Celerico, the guards were cantoned this day in Mello; General Howard's in Sampayo, the King's German legion in Gouvea, General Nightingall's in Villa Cortez and Cortiço. Head-quarters in Celerico. Massena occupied Guarda with a considerable force; indeed, the numbers of the retreating army are computed at nearly 50,000.

On the 29th the division marched to Celerico, and about sun-set the troops were quartered in the town and the neighbouring villages of Chesu, Lagiosa, Val de Sierras, Frontilhera, &c. The artillery at Baraçal. The principal arch of the bridge over the Mondego, had been destroyed, but was now repaired for the passage of the allied army.

Massena left Guarda this morning with one corps of his army and part of another, on the appearance of the British columns. General Picton with the 3d division, moved across the Sierra d'Estrella, upon the enemy's left, by the mountain track from Manteigas; the light division advanced upon the right from Fraxedas, while General Alexander Campbell marched upon the high road through the valley of the Mondego, and ascended the hill of Guarda in front of the city. This movement was so skilfully combined, that the heads of the several columns made their appearance on the heights of Guarda nearly at the same moment, and the celerity and precision of their manœuvres so intimidated the enemy, that without firing a gun, he immediately commenced his retreat towards the Coa, in the direction of Sabugal, pursued by the cavalry and light troops, who skirmished with the rear-guard and made about 300 prisoners.

As the French retired, the peasantry came with their implements of husbandry from their hiding places, and commenced their labours; in many places the vines were already trimmed, and the industrious farmer, busied in his fields, seemed anxious to repair the loss of time, and the devastation committed by the enemy.

March the 30th the division halted: on the following morning the guards marched 5 leagues to Fraxedas; the artillery and the King's German legion halted in Alverça, which during the sieges of Ciudad Rodrigo and Almeida, had been Lord Wellington's head-quarters; the route was through Celerico and Baraçal.

April the 1st the troops remained in their cantonments. At Fraxedas the enemy, in addition to their usual atrocities, violated the repose of the dead, by opening the graves in the church, which was in ruins, in hopes of finding valuables buried in the coffins.

April 2d. The army advanced towards the Coa, and the brigades of the 1st division were cantoned at night-fall, in villages about a league from the river.

April 3d. Soon after day-break, the army moved forward to attack the enemy in Sabugal, where General Regnier remained with the 2d *corps d'armee*. About mid-day the action commenced by a brisk cannonade, and the enemy being compelled to evacuate the town, drew up on an adjoining height, from whence they were dislodged by the light division in a most gallant manner, before the other troops could come into action. General Picton advanced 2 miles in front of the town, to the ground on which part of the enemy had *bivouaced*. The attack being entirely unexpected, their tents were left standing, and were taken possession of with a considerable quantity of baggage, the greater part of which, fell into the hands of the light division, whose conduct on this day, obtained the approbation and thanks of Lord Wellington, and the admiration of the whole army.

The light division was quartered this evening in Sabugal, and the principal part of the army got under cover in the adjoining villages, although some of the troops were necessarily obliged to *bivouac*.—Heavy rain during the greater part of the day.—Headquarters at the Quinta of Gonsalvo Martinez, in the Vale of Monrisco, from whence they moved next day into Sabugal. The guards were cantoned in the ruined village of St. Antonio, where they remained until the morning of the 5th, when the whole of the troops were again in motion. The guards, and Major-General Howard's brigade forded the Coa, a mile and a half above Sabugal. This little town, which is on the Spanish side of the river, is of great antiquity, and surrounded with a wall. The handsome Moorish tower is still in great preservation.

At noon, the 7th division passed through the column which then proceeded to Navé, in which town, the guards and Major-General Howard's brigade, halted for the night.

April 6th. The troops were in motion soon after day-light.—The guards, about 9 o'clock, passed through the ancient Moorish town of Alfaytes, and 2 hours afterwards, reached Aldea Velha, on the road to Villa Mayor.

On the following day to Turcalhos, one league.—Nearly the whole of the British army entered Spain.

April 8th. The guards halted, and on the 9th, advanced over the frontier through Albegaria, to the little village of Almadilla, 2 leagues from Villa Formosa—head quarters. The light division at the same time, moved forward to Gallegos, and occupied their former cantonments.

The French, when attacked on the 3d instant at Sabugal, were on the point of firing a *feu de joie* in honour of the birth of the King of Rome, the account of which had just been received from Paris.

After the action, Regnier made a forced march of 18 hours, and on the 4th, reached the Agueda, over which, the whole of the army destined for the subjugation of Portugal, had retired on the 8th instant.

The result of the operations, in which the British army has been engaged for the last five weeks, is highly satisfactory; not a Frenchman at this moment, remaining in the kingdom, with the exception of the garrison of Almeida, and the communication betwixt this fortress and Ciudad Rodrigo, is completely cut off; the combined army now occupying a line, the left of which rests upon the Douro.

Whilst the mode of warfare to which Lord Wellington restricted himself in the late pursuit of Massena, proved extremely embarrassing to the troops of the enemy, the British army having sustained few privations, and undergone no unnecessary fatigue, is in the highest health and spirits, unbroken, and ready to enter upon any further operations to which they may be called.—Massena's army on the contrary, is known to be disorganized and dispirited, and some weeks must elapse before it can be again in a condition to take the field. The accounts constantly received, of the distress which the French suffered in the position at Santarem, from a scarcity of provisions, and the consequent sickness of the troops, proved to be no exaggeration, and was fully confirmed by the inhabitants of these places occupied by the enemy, who, from a variety of causes, had remained in their homes. The French leader, apprehensive of being attacked on the arrival of the expected reinforcements from England, and fearing the consequences in the exhausted state of his army, at length determined upon a retreat, which was in fact, become a matter of imperious necessity.

However formidable the position of Santarem, the invincible spirit and superior discipline of British troops, must have ensured them complete success, whenever an attack was determined upon. The French army, for the purpose of foraging, occupied an extended line of country; and the force in the town was by no means adequate to maintain it, had a division of troops passed the Tagus in its rear, whilst the attention of the enemy was directed to points more immediately threatened, by which the principal part of the attacking columns, owing to local circumstances, must of necessity have approached. These considerations, and the distress of his army, had doubtless their weight on the mind of the French leader, who found himself in a situation of unexampled difficulty, to him " the spoiled child of victory," altogether new, and to extricate himself from which, required the exertion of all his talents, and of all his firmness. The reverse which the Prince of Essling has experienced in his attempts to subjugate Portugal, must be the more painful to his feelings, when he reflects, that he has for ever tarnished his military fame, by his vain, arrogant and premature boast in the face of the whole world, to drive the English into the sea, and plant the eagles of Napoleon on the towers of Lisbon.—To the last moment was the farce kept up, and his deluded troops endeavoured to forget their wants in hopes of the plunder of the metropolis, the sole object of their thoughts, for which they had made so many painful marches, and undergone the most severe privations. In the theatre at Santarem, which the French officers had fitted up for their amusement, the piece represented, on the eve of this memorable retreat, and brought out with every adventitious aid of scenery, calculated to dazzle the senses, and inflame the passions of the soldiery, was the " Frenchman in Lisbon !"

The most barbarous excesses were committed by the enemy throughout his whole line of march, and the inhabitants, who from age or sickness, were unable to quit their houses, became victims to the horrid brutality of the French soldiery. There is no atrocity of which these unprincipled ruffians have not been guilty: — every crime that stains the black catalogue of human cruelty having been committed on the persons and property of the poor wretches who had the misfortune to fall into their hands. The prospect before the advanced guard, was always that of burning villages, of plundered cottages, of murdered peasants.—The roads were covered with the dying and the dead—with cannon, baggage and ammunition, which the enemy could not carry off; with mutilated cattle, with every thing, in short, that could create horror and disgust, that could make the heart feel sentiments of indignation against the barbarous enemy, and of pity for the suffering and ravaged natives. Not unfrequently, however, the latter were able to revenge upon the invader, the cruelties he had committed. In some of the villages, the peasants had cut off detachments of the enemy, and put them to instant death.

Nearly the whole of the once beautiful city of Leyria is reduced to ashes. The mansion of the rich and the cottage of the poor, were alike the objects of the enemy's vengeance, and involved in one common conflagration by the merciless destroyer.

The magnificent convent of Alcobaça has been burnt by Massena's order, and Batalha would have shared the same fate, but for the massive strength of its walls, which resisted the sacrilegious attempt.

A strong detachment of the *corps d'armee*, which daily formed the rear guard of the retreating enemy, was specially allotted to carry the work of destruction into execution.

LETTER XLII.

Massena having collected the whole of the Troops in the North of Spain, makes an Attempt to relieve Almeida.—Battle of Fuentes de Honor.—Almeida abandoned by the Garrison.

Almadilla, 12*th May*, 1811.

LORD Wellington having learnt, that the Prince of Essling had assembled a council of war at Ciudad Rodrigo on the 1st instant, which was attended by 26 generals, and the enemy having for some days previously, made frequent demonstrations on the left bank of the Agueda, it was supposed that the French chief meditated an attempt to relieve Almeida, or failing in that to bring off the garrison, which was known to be now in much distress for provisions.

On the following day, the enemy crossed the river in force, and drove the light division out of Gallegos. The whole of the troops in consequence, moved from their cantonments, and on the 3d, this part of the army under the immediate command of Lord Wellington, was concentrated betwixt the Villages of

Fuentes de Honor in Spain, and Villa Fermosa in Portugal, two leagues from Almeida, and four from Ciudad Rodrigo.

In the course of the same day, the French army, commanded by Massena, having under him Marshals Marmont and Bessieres, and General Loison, arrived on the plains on the other side of Fuentes, the key of the British position, and about 2 in the afternoon, pushed forward several corps of sharpshooters to attack the village, which was defended with the greatest obstinacy by the light troops, but the enemy, from his superiority of numbers, at length obtained possession of this important post, from which, however, he was soon after dislodged by the 71st regiment, under Colonel Cadogan, at the point of the bayonet. This was a little before dusk. Next morning the enemy renewed his attacks upon the village, but every effort proved unsuccessful.

At day-break on the 5th, it was perceived that the enemy had moved the whole of his cavalry, and several heavy columns of infantry towards the right. About 6 o'clock, his manœuvres seemed to indicate an attack on that point, and soon after the cavalry, deriving confidence from their numbers, advanced upon the British, which was their weak arm, and compelled them to give way, but in retreating, the British cavalry repeatedly faced about, and made some successful charges upon the enemy. Meanwhile, the 7th division, which had been considerably advanced upon the plain, was directed to fall back and form on the brigade of guards posted on the right of the 1st division, and flanked by Captain Lawson's brigade of 9 pounders, and some squadrons of cavalry.

Their point d'Appui rested on some broken and rocky ground, intersected with inclosures of stone walls, and copse wood, having a small river the Turon, in the rear.

Major General Houston was enabled to execute this retrograde movement in the face of an infinitely superior force, principally by the steadiness and gallant conduct of the 2 foreign corps in his division, the Duke of Brunswick Oel's infantry, and the Chasseurs Brittanniques, under Lieutenant-Colonel Eustace, who checked the advance of the French cavalry, by several well directed vollies. The enemy had previous to this, opened a tremendous fire upon the first line of infantry; every shot that went over doing execution in the second line.

The light division, which at first formed on the left of the 7th division, also retired before the enemy's cavalry in echellon of squares, and in the finest order.

About 11 A. M. the picquet of the guards, consisting of 100 rank and file, under Lieutenant-Colonel Hill, skirmishing in front of the brigade, was charged by a squadron of cavalry, which they repulsed, and were retiring upon the 42nd regiment, commanded by Lord Blantyre, formed in columns for the support of the light troops upon some broken ground, when the enemy returned to the attack in such numbers, that after seeing most of his officers and men cut down, Colonel Hill being wounded, was compelled to surrender himself prisoner

Ensign Cookson was killed, Ensign Stothert of the Coldstream, wounded slightly and taken prisoner. — Captains Home and Harvey escaped, although for some minutes in the enemy's hands, the latter slightly wounded. At this moment, the 9 pounders having opened upon the French cavalry, they retired in great confusion. About the same time, the enemy pushed forward his light infantry upon the right, where they were met and repulsed by Colonel Guise, with the light companies of the guards and part of the 95th regiment, under Captain O'Hare.

The line was now formed with the 7th division on the right of the 1st division, having on its left General Crawford with the light division in reserve.—Beyond, were those of Major Generals Picton, A. Campbell and Sir William Erskine. The left of the whole was on Fort Conception, covering Almeida

The principal part of the cavalry remained on the right.—Brigadier-General Pack was stationed with the Queen's regiment, and a brigade of Portuguese infantry watching Almeida, from whence guns were fired at intervals as signals.

The 7th division subsequently crossed the Turon, and formed upon the hill in rear of the present line, on which, should Lord Wellington think proper to refuse his right, a new position was intended to be taken up.

The firing slackened on both sides towards the evening, but the engagement was not finally over until the close of day, when the enemy, who was repulsed at all points, remained in the same position as at the commencement of the action, being unable to gain a single advantage or make the smallest impression upon any part of the British line.

The French army is stated to have been not less than 40,000 infantry and 5000 cavalry when they entered the field. Their loss is estimated at from 1500 to 2000 killed; and it is known that 3500 wounded have been carried into Ciudad Rodrigo. Our loss has also been severe, amounting to 1760 in killed, wounded and missing; but this number falls short of what might have been expected from the length of time the troops were under fire.

The principal contest was in Fuentes, the possession of which was of the utmost importance to either army. Colonel Cameron was mortally wounded at the head of the 79th regiment in defending this village.

The hostile armies remained in front of each other on the two following days; and in the afternoon of the 7th, were employed in burying their dead. During this interval, working parties were constantly occupied in strengthening the position of the British, by throwing up field works.

The enemy having received a reinforcement, a renewal of the attack was generally expected on the morning of the 8th, instead of which, at day-break, his cavalry Videttes galloped off to the rear, and soon after, several columns of infantry appeared moving in the same direction. The French continued their retreat on the 9th, but a strong rear guard of about 2000 cavalry and several battalions of infantry remained in sight. On the 10th, the British broke up from their position, and while the light division, supported by the cavalry, advanced towards the Agueda; the rest of the army returned to cantonments, and the original investment of Almeida was resumed.

Colonel Trant arrived on the 7th, with a division of Portuguese, and the corps of Don Julian Sanchez took a share in the action, and checked the enemy's movements on the right.

Early on the morning of the 11th, the garrison of Almeida made a sortie, and cut their way to the Bridge of San Felices, through the British piquets, with the exception of 470, who were either killed, or wounded and taken. General Brenier, the Governor, had previously blown up several bastions, and the curtains next the Coa, and destroyed the guns of the fortress, with an immense quantity of stores in the arsenal, which was burnt.—The prisoners were mostly in a state of intoxication, which was also the case with the French cavalry on the 5th instant.

Soon after day-light, General Pack, with his brigade of infantry, entered Almeida. It appears that the French evacuated the town about midnight on the 10th, and having formed in column, waited near some ruined houses, a short distance from the walls, until the explosion took place. Their object was to destroy the reveltement or outer rampart, and the branches of the grand mine were conducted accordingly.

Anxious to ascertain the success of his labours, the commanding engineer remained behind, intending to follow the garrison on the Malpartida road, but he is said to have perished in one of the chambers, owing to which circumstance, the whole of the mines were not sprung. The bastions of the faces nearest the Coa were demolished, and the intervening curtain destroyed. The stone work of the ramparts fell into the ditch and part was carried completely over. No injury on this occasion, was done to the town, which had suffered most severely by the explosion of the grand magazine in August last, previous to its surrender to the French. In consequence of that event, Almeida became one vast heap of ruins, a great number of the garrison, and of the inhabitants perished; the south-west curtain sustained considerable damage, and few houses escaped, without receiving some material injury. Of the two magazines which were placed in the castle, the most elevated spot in Almeida, not one stone remained upon another, nor can the foundation of these buildings be now distinguished.

The enemy had been for some days previous to the 10th, employed in spiking the guns, and otherwise rendering them useless: the whole of the military stores were then collected in the arsenal and set on fire. It is here proper to remark, that the French shewed some degree of consideration for the remaining inhabitants of this devoted town, and they do not complain of any ill-treatment.

The campaign, by the fall of Almeida, may now be considered at an end, as far as regards Portugal; and the whole kingdom has again been delivered from the yoke of France, whose hitherto victorious legions, under the command of their ablest chiefs, have in every instance met with disgrace and defeat, when opposed to the British troops.

LETTER XLIII.

Operations of Marshal Sir William Beresford on the Guadiana.—Battle of Albuera.—General Lumley's brilliant Affair with the French Cavalry at Usagre.—The Siege of Badajos raised a second time.—The whole of the Allied Army in the Alentejo.—Lord Wellington in the beginning of August re-crosses the Tagus, and invests Ciudad Rodrigo, into which Marmont throws Supplies on the 24th of September, and advances over the Aqueda. —The Allied Army takes up a position in front of the Coa.—Marmont retires.

Pinhel, 5th December, 1811.

PREVIOUS to the commencement of Massena's retreat from Santarem, Marshals Soult and Mortier advanced from the south of Spain, in order to form a combined operation with *the army of Portugal.* In pursuance of this object the latter possessed himself of Merida on the 9th of January, and forthwith invested Badajos with his infantry, placing his cavalry on the right bank of the Guadiana.

General Mendizabel was dispatched to the relief of Badajos on the 20th of January, with the Spanish corps, which under the command of the Marquis de la Romana, had joined Lord Wellington in the lines, on the 19th of October. After some trifling manœuvres, the Spanish General threw himself into the city, from whence he again withdrew his army on the 9th of February, and took up a position on the ridge of St. Christoval, which commanded an extensive view in every direction. Notwithstanding this advantage, which appears to have been disregarded by General Mendizabel, the French army crossed the Gevora and Guadiana, surprised and totally defeated the Spaniards. The French cavalry pursued the fugitives (who as usual threw away their arms,) across the plain to the walls of Elvas, and captured the whole of the Spanish artillery and baggage.

The enemy was thus enabled to sit down quietly before Badajos; and M. Mortier lost no time in breaking ground and commencing the siege. A small breach having been made on the 10th, (but by no means practicable for assault, if properly defended,) the traitor Imaz, who succeeded to the command, on General Menacho being killed, lthough apprized that Marshal Beresford was marching to his relief, surrendered the city and a garrison equal in number to the enemy. General Menacho had made every disposition for defending the place to the last extremity; the streets were barricaded, and the garrison was well supplied with ammunition and provisions for a month.

The French had previously obtained possession of Olivenza and its garrison, consisting of 3000 Spaniards; but a Portuguese force of only 250 men bravely defended the fortress of Campo Mayor from the 14th to the 21st of March. On the 25th Marshal Beresford having been reinforced by the Honourable Major-General Cole's division of infantry, advanced against Campo Mayor, which the enemy abandoned on the appearance of the British and Portuguese cavalry. Two squadrons of the 13th dragoons, and two squadrons of Portuguese charged the French cavalry, who were broke and pursued to Badajos, but the infantry effected their retreat to the fortress in a solid body, although with considerable loss, and recovered the cannon which had been taken by the allied cavalry. It was unfortunate that the infantry were not combined in this operation, as the capture or destruction of the enemy would have been completely effected with their assistance.

After this affair, Sir William Beresford threw a bridge over the Guadiana at Jurumenha, and in the course of the 4th and 5th of April he crossed with his army; then leaving General Cole's division to attack Olivenza, he advanced with the whole of his remaining force, and drove the enemy (who did not think it expedient to risk an action.) into the Sierra Morena. Having accomplished this object, and Olivenza having surrendered to the Honourable Major-General Cole on the 15th of April, Marshal Beresford returned to undertake the siege of Badajos, which place was completely invested on the 7th of May by the allied army, and a Spanish corps commanded by Don Carlos D'Espagne. On the following day the batteries were opened against Fort St. Christoval, and the garrison returned a very brisk fire upon the besiegers. Sir William Beresford having received information on the 12th that Marshal Soult was advancing from Seville, dispatched a courier to Lord Wellington with that intelligence; and judging it necessary to suspend his operations against Badajos, the heavy field train was sent back to Elvas.

Lord Wellington lost no time in reinforcing Marshal Sir William Beresford with the 3d and 7th divisions of infantry, under Generals Picton and Houston, and proceeded himself to Elvas, which his Lordship reached on the 19th instant.—Meantime, however, the battle of Albuera was fought on the heights, above the village of that name; and Marshal Soult was completely repulsed by the allied British and Portuguese army, under Sir William Beresford, and a corps of 10,000 Spaniards, commanded by Generals Blake and Castanos. The superior numbers of the enemy's cavalry enabled him to make good his retreat towards Seville, which he commenced on the morning of the 18th, two days after the action. The Honourable General Lumley followed them with the British and Portuguese cavalry to Usagre, where the enemy having collected a considerable force, attacked the allied cavalry on the 26th instant. Major-General Lumley had previously retired through Usagre, and having posted his troops on some favourable ground behind that village, waited the enemy's attack. Three regiments dashed through Usagre in a very resolute manner, but had scarcely formed when they were charged by General De Grey's brigade of heavy cavalry, and completely overturned. The French cavalry immediately broke and fled, leaving a number of prisoners, and killed and wounded on the field.—The nature of the country did not permit General Lumley to follow up the advantage he had so happily gained, and with a very trifling loss.

The siege of Badajos was now resumed, and on the 2d of June batteries were re-opened against Fort St. Christoval and the body of the place. A breach having been effected in Fort St. Christoval, an attempt was made on the 6th of June to carry the work, and subsequently, on the night of the 9th, both of which failed, and the besiegers retired with loss.

Before day-break, on the 6th of June, the guards once more marched from Almadilla, and passing through Aldea de Ponte, arrived about 8 A. M. at the miserable village of Robilosa, where they halted until noon. The brigade then marched by Alfayates to Soita, and *bivouaced* about a mile beyond.

At 4 in the morning of the 7th, the guards at the head of the 1st division moved off to Sabugal, and crossing the Coa at the bridge, took up a position on the left bank of the river, and threw out strong piquets to protect the fords. In the course of the day the light division and the 6th arrived on this ground. This movement was occasioned by the enemy having pushed forward a considerable body of cavalry and some infantry in front of Ciudad Rodrigo, on which Sir Brent Spencer withdrew his outposts, expecting to be attacked on the 7th or 8th by the whole of the enemy's force in that quarter.—These operations of the French leader Marshal Marmont, (who had succeeded to the command of the army on Massena's recal to Paris,) appear to have been made with a view of masking his real intention; for early in the afternoon of the 8th it was ascertained that the enemy was moving in force towards the pass of Banos. The troops were then directed to proceed to the Alentejo, and on the 14th and 15th the column crossed the Tagus at the romantic pass of Villa Velha, over a flying bridge.—Lieutenant Johnston of the royal artillery, was unfortunately drowned while trying this ford.

On the 16th the brigade entered Portalegre, in which city the 6th and light division were also quartered; and on the 19th the 1st division marched to Assumar, and the light division to Aronches. On the 23d the guards advanced to St. Olaya, and hutted near that town.

Previous to this period the Commander of the forces had again raised the siege of Badajos, the enemy having assembled the whole of his disposable force in Estremadura, and still retaining a considerable superiority in cavalry over the British. On the 22d the enemy advanced 40 squadrons of his cavalry and some field-pieces, for the purpose of making a *reconnoissance ;* but although they carried off a picquet of the 11th dragoons, commanded by Captain Lutyens, yet on the appearance of the British and Portuguese cavalry, the French retired into Badajos, without having seen the position of the allied army, the right of which rested upon Elvas, the line extending along a ridge, intersected by the small river Caya, towards the fortress of Campo Mayor, in which the 7th division of the army was quartered. The main body of the allied army was in huts.

In the beginning of July Marshal Soult leaving from 6 to 7000 men in Badajos, placed his army in cantonments, having his head-quarters at Asugal; Marmont at Truxillo; and Regnier in Merida.

The British and Portuguese army continued in camp until the 24th of July, and then moved into quarters. The Commander of the forces and heads of departments in Portalegre.—The 28th of July being the anniversary of the battle of Talavera, an entertainment was given at head-quarters, and a ball in the evening, which was attended by General Castanos and his suite, the officers in garrison, and some of the principal inhabitants of this city.

Marmont having passed the Tagus and established himself at Placentia; in the beginning of August the main body of the British army recrossed the river at Villa Velha, and the Commander of the forces fixed his head-quarters at Fuente Guinaldo, about 2 leagues from Ciudad Rodrigo. Part of the infantry was pushed forward on the Salamanca road, and all communication cut off betwixt the fortress and the enemy.

As it was known in the early part of September that a convoy was preparing at Salamanca, destined for the relief of Ciudad Rodrigo, the combined forces were assembled on the line of the Agueda on the 23d of that month. About 2 P. M. on the following day, the head of the convoy was observed entering the fortress, and in the course of the same night the whole arrived. For its protection, the enemy had assembled a large army, consisting of 55,000 infantry and 6000 cavalry. Of this force, General Baraguay D'Hillier's Count D'Orsenne brought 22,000 from Salamanca, and the remainder were the divisions under Marmont; which, since their retiring from Estremadura, had been cantoned at Placentia, Talavera de la Reyna, and other towns on the Upper Tagus. Previous to the enemy's approach, the British out-posts were withdrawn to the left bank of the Agueda; over which, the enemy pushed his advanced guard, 2 regiments of cavalry and 3000 infantry, on the evening of the 24th.

Next day at noon the enemy moved a force upon the 3d division, Major-General Picton's, which remained in a strong position on the right bank of the Azava, and the French cavalry advancing in considerable numbers, took 2 pieces of Portuguese artillery after cutting down the men at their guns. The 5th regiment then charged in the most gallant stile, retook these 2 pieces and subsequently retired with the 77th regiment in one square, and the 19th Portuguese regiment forming another before the French cavalry, who repeatedly charged three faces of the British square without effect. This manœuvre was directed by the Honourable

Major-General Colville; and the 11th light dragoons, commanded by Colonel Cumming, and German hussars succeeded in keeping the immensely superior force of the enemy in check.

About 3 o'clock the enemy appeared in front of Carpio, and his movements having manifested a design upon that village, a place of no importance, Major-General Alexander Campbell withdrew the 6th division behind the Duas Casas to the woods in front of Nave d'Aver.

On the 26th of September, all was quiet, and the enemy in motion to the right. He also shewed a force in front of Fuente Guinaldo, and deployed in view of the British already drawn up in line under the immediate orders of Lord Wellington; but after some time he relinquished his intended attack, and having re-formed his columns, continued his movement to the right.

At 3 in the morning of the 27th of September, the 1st division marched through Villa Mayor to Bismula, which they reached before noon, and at 10 P. M. the troops were again in motion and made a night march to Rendo, which they passed about 4 in the morning and halted in a wood half a mile beyond. Heavy rains for some hours.

In this position, the left of the ground on which the Commander of the forces had determined to meet the threatened attack of the enemy, the 1st division remained until the following day, and then crossed the Coa to take up cantonments in the valley of the Mondego, agreeably to General Graham's orders, dated Rendo, 28th of September, 1811.

The Lieutenant-General has received the orders of his Excellency the Commander of the forces, to march the troops into cantonments, as the enemy has abandoned the attempt of attacking the army in this position. He is confident that the left could not have been forced, defended by such troops as he has the honour to command.

The position extended from Rendo to Soita across the high road and covering Sabugal, both flanks resting on the Coa, having several fords and bridges in its rear for the retreat of the troops, in the event of an unsuccessful conflict.

In the middle of October, Don Julian Sanchez, ever on the alert, carried off a large proportion of the cattle belonging to the garrison of Ciudad Rodrigo, and made prisoner the Governor General Reynaud, the same officer who commanded the rear-guard of Soult's army when driven from Oporto.

At 1 in the morning of the 2d of November, an order arrived for the 1st division to move up to the frontier, and at the same time, the whole army was put in motion. At 9 o'clock, the order to march was cancelled, the new Governor of Ciudad Rodrigo having reached that town with some provisions, under an escort of 4000 men.

Accounts were received at head-quarters of Lieutenant-General Hill having completely surprised a division of the 5th corps at Arroya Molinas, commanded by General Girard, who was wounded and escaped with difficulty. The whole of his baggage, artillery, and upwards of 1000 prisoners, including the Duke D'Aremberg and General Brone were taken.

The army was again advanced to the frontier in the latter end of November, intelligence having been received, that the enemy intended to throw supplies into Ciudad Rodrigo. This movement was also supposed to have for its object, the protection of Almeida from insult during the repair of the fortifications.

The army remained for a few days in this position, and then moved into winter quarters. Lord Wellington returned to Freneda, and the head-quarters of the 1st division were fixed at Pinhel.

No place or territory had suffered more, in consequence of the French invasion, than the city and bishoprick of Pinhel. The furniture of the bishop's palace was entirely destroyed, but this noble pile of building remained entire. The Franciscan monastery, and now deserted convent of Ursulines, had been occupied successively, by French, English and Portuguese troops, and received considerable injury. The town within the walls, is evidently of great antiquity, and the fine Moorish castle must have been impregnable in former ages. In one of its towers is a small circular building, supposed to contain a flight of steps leading to some subterranean dungeons, but from the present state of the walls, it is impossible to ascertain the exact use for which it was originally intended. A beautiful antique cross ornaments the market place.

The venerable bishop, who resides at the Quinta of St. Euphemia, 2 leagues distant, made the following affecting report of the devastation committed in his diocese, to the regency.

The local position of the bishoprick of Pinhel, on the confines of this kingdom, containing in its bounds, the fortress of Almeida and the military road to the province of Leon, from the interior of Portugal, has placed it in the melancholy necessity of serving as the theatre of preparation for the defence of the kingdom, from the beginning of the fatal war of the French revolution; for the formation of a military road at the time of the intrusion of French despotism, and for the march of Sir John Moore, when his army entered the province of Leon, and latterly, since the beginning of the year 1810 to the following July, it constantly served as a position for the allied army as long as it remained in the province of Beira. On the march of that army into Estremadura, its toal ruin began with the entry of the hostile army, and from the latter being stationary in the territory of Pinhel, from July to the 13th of September, when it advanced into Estremadura, and ultimately, in its precipitate and furious retreat to Spain, being in the interim, from July to April, occupied and trodden in all parts, by different divisions of the enemy, marching to avoid the main army, or acting in flying parties through the bishoprick, sometimes in one part, sometimes in another; robbing and ravaging; inasmuch that, according to the most exact information, there is not a village which does not exhibit the marks of French wickedness in a manner more or less horrible.

It must likewise be observed, that the territory of Pinhel had previously suffered by the passage of the Gallician army to Leon, and during the war, by the marches and military evolutions of different divisions of Portuguese militia, at the time they were ordered to observe the enemy.

All these circumstances have concurred to

swell the volume of the public and private misfortunes of Pinhel to such a degree, that in this melancholy point of view, it infinitely outdoes all the other bishopricks of this kingdom, when the variety of armies and their divisions which have been stationary, and the still longer stay the enemy made in it are considered. The riches of the district, and the subsistence of its inhabitants, depend on the cultivation of corn and breeding cattle, and as these two articles, however much wanted for the allied army, became still greater objects of French rapine, it is now without sheep, oxen and corn, (consisting of rye and barley) and consequently without subsistence.

Exclusive of these evils proceeding from human causes, the bishoprick of Pinhel labours under others; for besides the epidemic fevers, which have carried off a great proportion of its inhabitants, those who remain have little hope from their scanty farms badly worked, and so devastated by the enemy, that they produce nothing, and in the memory of man never was there a more unproductive season for the few lands that have been cultivated.

The population of Pinhel was computed at from 30 to 40,000, it is now reduced to two thirds; the remainder being carried off by violent and natural deaths, and by emigration; such *is its present condition.*

The preceding observations of this respected prelate, may be applied with great truth, to the other provinces of this kingdom, which have been infested by the presence of the enemy.

Pinhel had only been recently erected into a bishop's see. There is at present, no establishment of canons or a cathedral, for which the ground is marked out, but the war has put a stop to the work. General Graham's quarters are in the bishop's palace, a magnificent quadrangular structure, having a large court in the centre.

Pinhel in former times, when the Spaniards possessed Almeida, and the whole country on the right bank of the Coa, must have been a place of great importance, nature having evidently marked it out as the frontier town of Portugal. The district betwixt the Coa and the Pinhel river is very rocky, and appears unsusceptible of cultivation.

LETTER XLV.

General remarks on the successful Campaign of 1811,—Observations respecting the Spanish Guerillas, &c.

Pinhel, 20th December, 1811.

THE recent successes of Lord Wellington, cannot fail of producing a beneficial effect upon the minds of the Spaniards, by encouraging a continuance of their efforts, to resist the progress of the invader, but must also be regarded with a corresponding interest, by the other nations of Europe, who have been hitherto led to consider the troops of Napoleon invincible. If roused by the moral feeling which these glorious events seem most forcibly calculated to inspire, the powers of the continent, should shake off the apathy, with which they have too long beheld the strides of the modern Alexander, and laying aside those pretty contemptible jealousies of each other, which Buonaparte has but too successfully promoted as the means of increasing his own power, then there is yet a hope, that the tyrant may be hurled from his throne, and the genius of liberty once more erect his standard on the Continent of Europe.

To the powerful influence which the disgrace of Massena must produce on the cause of Spain, and in the eyes of its inhabitants, is to be added the high character obtained in the course of the late operations, by the Portuguese. Two years have scarcely elapsed, since these troops, which now shine so conspicuously in the defence of their country, were an un-armed, ill-cloathed, un-accoutred, un-disciplined rabble, now they possess in an eminent degree, the best qualities of warriors, and have proved themselves " worthy of contending in the same " ranks with British soldiers." This happy object has been accomplished by the liberal policy of taking 30,000 Portuguese into British pay, and placing them under British officers of experience and talent. The measure has been crowned with such complete success, that it appears most desirable to extend this system over the whole Peninsula.

The population of Spain even in its present state is fully adequate to maintain an army of 200,000 men, independent of the Guerilla force, and of that number 30 or 40,000 might be taken into British pay, and trained by British officers on the same footing as the Portuguese. In the formation of these troops a due regard would of course be had to the character and feelings of this high-minded people. A proportion of British superior officers in no instance exceeding one half, should be allotted to each regiment, and this distribution might tend to prevent any jealousies arising among men although of different nations, yet fighting under the same standard, and united in one glorious cause. Those officers who have served in the peninsula, and have acquired a knowledge of the Spanish language and national character should of course be preferred to assist in the formation of these levies, the establishment of which is in perfect unison with the wise and extended policy hitherto pursued in the conduct of the present war, and the necessity of meeting the efforts of the enemy with increased means, becomes every day more apparent. But situated as Spain is at this moment, with nearly all her strong places in the enemy's possession, it would be found extremely difficult to organize and form regular bodies of troops, which after such training might be led with a prospect of success against the veteran legions of France. To promote habits of discipline, subordination and the other qualities requisite in the composition of a soldier's character, a length of time is necessary, and the quiet of a garrison at a distance from the actual theatre of war. In Gallicia, while it remains free from the enemy's presence, depôts might be found for the new levies; but, should the system above alluded to be adopted, the frontiers of Portugal seem peculiarly pointed out for the reception and formation of Spanish battalions in the pay of Britain.

At present, the only troops in Spain, which carry on a successful warfare against the French, are the Guerillas, or armed peasantry, and it may be fairly presumed, that they are incited to attack the enemy's convoys, and straggling parties, as much by the hope of plunder, as from motives of patriotism. This cannot be supposed to influence the minds of their gallant chiefs, but the peasant, when compelled by the ravages of war to abandon the scenes of peaceful industry, when no longer able to pursue his usual avocations, becomes of necessity a soldier, and assumes the military character, as the only means of supporting his existence. It is of these materials that the Guerilla force is principally composed, a hardy peasantry, despising danger and enduring the vicissitudes of the seasons, and every species of fatigue and privation with the fortitude of ancient Romans; minutely acquainted with the almost impenetrable recesses of their native land, its deep extensive forests and distant glens, the situation of its rivers and the devious paths which lead to their mountain holds, above all, receiving early intelligence of every movement made by the foe; it is not surprising therefore, that such a body sudden, and determined in attack, should carry terror and dismay, even into the ranks of the French soldiery, who have on numerous occasions, suffered most severely in their conflicts with these self-formed bands, some of which constantly hover in the neighbourhood of the capital, and at times, appearing before the gates of Madrid, alarm the usurper in the very moment of fancied security. But it is perfectly evident that the deliverance of Spain, can never be atchieved by the efforts of a force so rudely constituted, however useful it may be, and successful as it has often proved against small parties of the enemy in their desultory, yet impetuous attacks.

The armies which have overrun the continent and have raised the character of France as a military nation, beyond any former period of its history, can only be successfully opposed by troops of a similar description inured to habits of regular warfare, and accustomed to undergo the greatest hardships of which the human frame is capable. With an army thus organized, commanded by officers of approved merit, and possessing the confidence of their troops, Spain, aided by the vast resources of Great Britain, may yet anticipate a favourable result to the present contest, and finally accomplish the expulsion of the modern barbarians and their sanguinary leaders beyond the Pyrenees.

THE END.

www.ingramcontent.com/pod-product-compliance
Lightning Source LLC
Chambersburg PA
CBHW031136160426
43193CB00008B/157